100 DAYS IN HEAVEN

"After these things I looked, and behold, a door standing open in heaven. And the first voice which I heard was like a trumpet speaking with me, saying, "Come up here, and I will show you things which must take place after this." **(Revelation 4:1)**

James A. Durham

ACKNOWLEDGEMENTS

The entire contents of this book came as gifts from the Lord. Therefore, I want to express my thanks first and foremost to Him for providing the revelation for this book and for the inspiration along the way to complete the project. The Lord is good and His love and mercy endure forever. Without Him none of our works would succeed. It is with gratitude and praise that I acknowledge all He has done to make this book possible.

I want to acknowledge the invaluable assistance I received from my extremely blessed, highly favored, and anointed wife, Gloria. Without her encouragement and assistance this book could never have been completed. I am also grateful for her dedicated and tireless assistance in proof reading the book and confirming the accuracy of the scriptural references. I also want to acknowledge my daughter, Michelle, who remains a constant and consistent cheerleader throughout the process of all my writings. Anytime I needed encouragement, I had only to turn to either of these two wonderful ladies. I am so thankful to the Lord that He placed them in my life and constantly blesses me through their love and support!

I am also grateful to the many people who received the daily emails during the three years, four months and two weeks of this assignment from the Lord. Many of you responded to the messages and gave me encouragement by sharing testimonies about receiving what the Lord was releasing and turning all these things into ministry. Thank you for sharing testimonies of healings, miracles, signs and wonders. Thank you for your encouragement and support. You have each been a blessing and inspiration to me and I will always be grateful. I hope these messages will be a blessing to many of you, because so few of the recipients of the "What Heaven is Saying Today" daily emails ever saw the messages in this book.

PREFACE

I n the Fall of 2008, we attended the Harvest Fest Conference at MorningStar in Fort Mill, SC. During one of the worship services as very loud music was being release by the worship team, I was lifted up to Heaven for an extended visit and received a life changing experience with the Lord. What I experienced in that visit to Heaven gave me an entirely new outlook on ministry and the teachings of the Bible about the second coming of Jesus. I was sitting very straight in the chair which was a very comfortable position for an experience like the one I was given. I had my hands palms down on top of my legs when the Spirit lifted me up to an open portal into Heaven.

As I looked up through the open portal, something like dark clouds repeatedly moved across to block my view into Heaven. I knew this was a move by the enemy to prevent me from having this experience. I repeated the words of James 4:7, "Therefore submit to God. Resist the devil and he will flee from you." After I spoke this verse, the clouds dispersed and I was able to see through the portal again. Then the clouds came back to block my view. This happened several times and I realized that the enemy is very persistent in his attempts to block us from receiving what the Lord has for us. So, I pressed in until I moved past the clouds. I was then in the middle of the portal with my head and shoulder above it and my feet below it.

At this point, I saw a small red light moving overhead from left to right. It seemed very high above me and I watched it slowly moving overhead. Then the Lord asked, "Do you want that?" I wasn't sure what it was, but felt confident in asking for it since the Lord was releasing it in Heaven. I said, "Yes!" Then the Lord motioned with His eyes toward my left hand which was palm down on my left leg. At this point, I was very detached in my spirit from my body. I was aware that my body was still in the worship center, but it seemed very far away. From the motion by Jesus, I knew that I had to turn my hand over and lift it upward to receive what the Lord was releasing. That proved to be very difficult because of my detachment from the body. It seemed like I was moving a ton of weight in that hand. I finally achieved the goal and was ready to receive what the Lord was giving.

The little red light moved toward my hand and I could finally see exactly what it was. As it got closer, it looked larger. When it came into my hand, I could see that it was a very large ruby about the size of an egg. I was delighted to receive it and to see it in my hand. It was so real to my eyes and my touch that I expected to still have it when the experience in Heaven was over. I asked the Lord, "What is it?" He replied, "It is the love of the Father coming to you as a gift for your ministry." As I watched the ruby, it began to merge or melt into the palm of my hand. Then I knew this was a spiritual manifestation rather than something I would have in the natural. As it continued to merge with my left hand, I asked the Lord, "Shouldn't this be in my right hand so that I can impart it to others?" The Lord responded, "When you stand face to face and impart it to others, you will place it in their right (correct) hand. Remember that your heart is on your left side and this is the correct place for you to carry this gift from the Father." The Ruby continued to melt into my hand and I suddenly felt extreme heat in that hand.

As I processed what I had received, I saw something moving above toward my right hand. The Lord asked, "Do you want that one too?" As I looked at this one, I saw that it was a dull colored black looking stone. It was not shining, and I wasn't really sure if I wanted this one. However, the Lord was offering it and I decided that I should take it. Then the Lord gestured toward my right hand which was still face down on my leg, and said, "Well?" Again, I had great difficulty turning my hand over and raising it up to receive this gift from the Lord. I learned from this experience to always have my hands open and uplifted when I go into His presence.

As this object came close to my hand, I could see it more clearly. I was very surprised to see that it was a lump of coal. In many old American Christmas stories and songs, the naughty children receive a lump of coal in their stockings from Santa Claus. I hoped that there was a different meaning for this stone. I asked the Lord to tell me what it meant, and He said, "It is a diamond in the rough. As you minister in the Kingdom, it will continuously be polished and eventually be clearly seen as a diamond of great value." This really sounded good. So, I welcomed this gift from the Lord. However, I was surprised when it landed in the palm of my hand. It began to burn like fire in my hand, and I felt the roughness of the stone wearing against my skin constantly for over two years.

The burning in both of my hands was constant day and night for more than two years. The pain from the fire of the Lord was sometimes almost unbearable. I would place my hands under cold running water to cool them down, but as soon as I pulled my hands from the water, the burning would almost instantly come back to full intensity. My wife experienced this same thing. This reassured me of something I understood from the Lord. Everything I receive in these Third Heaven visits is also available to others who hear about them or read about them and are willing to receive what the Lord is releasing. The fire still comes and goes in my hands and in my wife's hands after all this time. This almost always accompanies our ministry in the anointing. We have also seen many people receive the fire after hearing the testimony. Remember Revelation 19:10b, *"For the testimony of Jesus is the spirit of prophecy."*

After receiving both stones, the Lord lifted me up into Heaven. Together we flew about 50 feet in the air over many miles of the landscape of Heaven. My goal was to see the Holy City. This was such a powerful longing in my heart, but it would not be met in this visit. I traveled with the Lord over miles and miles of rolling hills with beautiful valleys surrounding them on all sides. There was a roadway between the mountains with crossroads in every valley. However there were no people anywhere in all the miles we travelled. I asked the Lord to help me understand. At first, I did not receive a response. We just continued to travel for a very long distance. Finally, we came to a beautiful river lined with trees on both sides. I knew what this was and it was so exciting to see it. You probably know what it is as well.

> *"Then the angel showed me the river of the water of life, as clear as crystal, flowing from the throne of God and of the Lamb down the middle of the great street of the city. On each side of the river stood the tree of life, bearing twelve crops of fruit, yielding its fruit every month. And the leaves of the tree are for the healing of the nations."*
> (Revelation 22:1-2, NIV)

We continued to fly along the path of the river for many miles as it took a winding path through the countryside. In all the miles we travelled, I did not see one single person on the ground or near the river. It was beautiful and I wanted to go down and soak in the water, but that also had to wait for another visit. I asked the Lord once again to help me understand the meaning of this experience. Finally, He revealed it to me and I received it with mixed emotions. I was very happy to get an understanding of what all of this meant, but the answer caused a very deep pain in my spirit. The Lord said, "This is the unoccupied part of Heaven. It should be filled with people, but my church has not done its job. The people who were to live here have never been reached by the Gospel of the Kingdom. They were never given a chance to accept it and come to their heavenly home!"

When I heard that, I began to weep bitterly. Then I knew why I had received those two stones and I knew why I felt so much pain from carrying them. I had to have that love of God in my heart to realize how much pain the Lord felt because of lost souls. Now I knew it in my limited capacity and the pain was almost overwhelming. I felt a great sense of responsibility for part to these empty spaces. A great desire to win the lost rose up from deep within my heart. This almost unbearable heartache for the lost continues to this very day. That is why I said that this was a life changing experience for me. The fire in my hands was so intense that I could not forget this Word from the Lord for even a few minutes. I continue to feel the pain and my desire to win the lost continues to this day. I pray that you will receive this intense fire, pain and desire from the Lord as you read the messages in this book.

As I wiped the tears from my eyes, I saw a great light in the distance. My first thought was that it was the light coming from the Holy City. I was being moved toward this glorious light or it was moving toward me. I didn't really know which because my eyes were so filled with tears. I didn't notice at this point that I was now accompanied by an angel rather than the Lord. My excitement began to build at the possibility of seeing the Holy City. The pain I was feeling in my heart was being slightly replaced by joy and excitement at what I was about to see. When the amazing light of His glory got closer I was able to see that this was coming from the Lord Jesus and a great company of the white robed army of the Lord. The light of His glory was so strong that I could hardly see details because I had to keep my eyes almost closed in the brightness of His radiance.

When the Lord got very close, I heard Him speak with great power and great authority, "I am coming very soon, and my

100 Days In Heaven

people are not ready!" Wow! That pronouncement was painful to hear. All I could think about was how to warn the people to get ready for His return. I felt almost powerless to deal with this information. What could I do to let people know what the Lord said? Then He spoke again in almost the same words, "Behold! I am coming very soon, and my church is not prepared!"

As this vision was ending, the Lord showed me the front cover of a book. I had never heard of this book before, but I could see the cover in crystal clarity. The title was, "The Power to Change the World: The Welsh and Azusa Street Revivals." I knew I had to get a copy as soon as possible, but had no idea where to find it. As I reoriented my eyes to the room, I looked up on the screen and to my great surprise and relief the book cover was being displayed on the screen. It was written by Rick Joyner and was on sale in the bookstore. I rushed to get a copy and could not put it down until the middle of the night when I finished reading it. The message in the book was another life changing experience for me. I purchased another copy and gave it to a discouraged missionary from Japan. He read it and was immediately strengthen to go back to the mission field he was about to abandon. Over time, I purchased several other copies and gave them to the people the Lord put into my spirit.

During the months that followed this experience, I had several other significant visits to the Third Heaven and received revelation for many things I was to do for the Lord. I was told to write a book about these experiences and under the Lord's direction wrote, "Beyond the Ancient Door: Free to Move about the Heavens." During several Third Heaven visits the Lord gave me the titles of all the chapters and an outline for each. As it was time to write the chapters, the Lord gave me another vision to go with each.

On January 3, 2010, during a Third Heaven visit, the Lord told me to quit using my nickname, Jim, and begin to use my legal name, James. He said that this was to happen because I was receiving a new anointing to visit the Third Heaven daily

xii

and send out the messages He gave me. The contents of this book were given to me during that year and I sent them out to a small number of people as the Lord directed. Later the Lord told me to select some of these messages and put them in this book so that others could receive them. He assured me that the messages are still appropriate for this time and in this season.

I did not try to organize these messages by their content or categorize them under certain titles. I am giving them in the order in which they came to me. They were obviously ahead of their time, because this is the time for their release. I did not include every message, but only the ones the Lord put into my heart. Many of the messages repeated the Lords decree, "Behold I am coming very soon!" Between these messages others were given as instructions from the Lord about how we are to get ready and stay alert during these days before His imminent return. I suggest that you read them in the same way the Lord gave them to me: one each day!

I pray that you will be as blessed by them as I have been in receiving them. May the Lord give you an outpouring of what He promised in Isaiah 11:2, *"The Spirit of the Lord shall rest upon Him, the Spirit of wisdom and understanding, the Spirit of counsel and might, the Spirit of knowledge and of the fear of the Lord."* Remember that Jesus prayed for us to receive the same love, glory and anointing He received from the Father for His earthly ministry. May we pick up the challenge and get busy sharing the good news of the Gospel of the Kingdom with the lost souls throughout the world! Amen? Even so, come quickly Lord Jesus!

DAY 1

A TIME OF SHAKING

After a time of worship and praise, I went face down on the floor; praying for the Holy Spirit to teach me what heaven is saying today. I began to see portals into heaven. I heard three times that we are in a season of open heavens. I heard the Spirit say, "Just reach up and take what you need!" I immediately stretched out my hand toward heaven to receive whatever Father God wants me to have. Before I go on, I want you to know that I understood these messages are for all of us and not just for me. I quickly reflected on others and asked that you be allowed to experience these same spiritual opportunities.

Then, I heard the Spirit say, "Why don't you just come up here and receive it!" Immediately, I found myself standing at the foot of the Tree of Life. I heard a voice saying, "The leaves are for the healing of the nations." So, I began to pluck leaves and stuff them into my pockets. I wanted to bring back all the healing power that I could carry. I desired an opportunity to take it to the nations. As I was stuffing my pockets, I ate a few leaves myself.

I didn't want to make the mistake of Joash who only struck the ground three times and limited the number of times God would act on his behalf. So, I continued to stuff my pockets with leaves until they would hold no more. Then I imagined that I had more pockets and stuffed them as well. At this point, I began to look for the fruit on the tree. I know that this tree produces fruit every month. I asked to know which fruit is in season now. I was told that this is the season of "peach-apples." (Perhaps some of you can add the prophetic meaning of combining peaches and apples). Then I saw one. It was large and very attractive. It looked like both a firm peach and an apple. I reached out, took it from the branch, and bit into it. I sensed both the flavor of a peach and an apple. It was firm, juicy, and very delicious.

Before I could focus on the texture and flavors I began to shake. The shaking started with my head and gradually moved down my body to my toes. The shaking increased in intensity until it became very violent. I sensed that things were being shaken off of me. I knew in my spirit that a remnant of the spirit of religion came off of me with numerous other fragments. It was a very freeing experience. I thank Father God for doing this for me and for making it available to you!

I started to feel an intense flow of energy pulsing from my mouth through my head and down my body in waves. It was a wonderful feeling of life, energy, love, healing, and power. I continued to shake violently with this flow which started with that first bite from the peach-apple. I sensed that this was a supernatural flow of living waters. It was a powerful flow of the river of life which was somehow coming from the fruit of the tree.

After a time, the shaking subsided. Then, I took another bite from the peach-apple, and it started up again. The intensity didn't increase, but it was extended over a longer period of time. I felt purged and cleansed in a new and powerful way. It was like being born again, again. Or like another baptism in the Holy Spirit. It was and is awesome.

When I returned from this visit to heaven, I was exhausted in a good way, and gasping for air. I continued to feel the pulsing flow of the energy of God throughout my body. I experienced something like chills of static electricity that continue even now. It continues to pulse around me and in me from my head to my toes.

I questioned whether to share this with others or not, but was quickly reminded that I had prayed for a word from heaven for you. In obedience, I release it with this suggestion. While we are in a season of open heavens, reach up and take what you need. Better still, go up and receive it. Remember what Paul wrote in Ephesians 2:6 (NIV), "*And God raised us up with Christ and seated us with him in the heavenly realms in Christ Jesus,*" Also reflect on Ephesians 2:18, "*For through Him* (Christ Jesus) *we both have access by one Spirit to the Father.*" Place a claim on your Biblical authority given in these two passages, and make a visit while the portals are open.

———————————

DAY 2

LIVING WATER FOR YOU

This morning, I received a marvelous vision. I was standing on the side of a hill overlooking a very large and beautiful lake. The area around me was covered with green grass like a well-manicured lawn in early spring. Trees lined the area and covered the shore of the lake. In front of me, I saw a very old-style water well. It had a circular stone wall in very good condition with wooden beams supporting a pulley system at the top. By turning the handle of the pulley system, I was able to bring the water to the surface. Then I heard these words from the book of Revelation:

> *"And He said to me, "It is done! I am the Alpha and the Omega, the Beginning and the End. I will give of the fountain of the water of life freely to him who thirsts."* (Revelation 21:6)

I dipped a cup into the bucket and retrieved a full cup of water. As I took a long refreshing drink from the cup, I was caught up in the experience. The water was cool, refreshing, flavorful, and living. It was nothing like the chlorinated water available in our homes and offices. It didn't have that slight plastic taste from bottled water. It had a familiar mineral flavoring. As I tasted the water, I was immediately transported back to the days of my youth when I visited friends who lived on farms and drank water from open wells. Memories of drawing cool refreshing water from the wells flooded my mind.

Then a revelation came. We are being offered living water by our Lord. Many of us have never tasted that kind of water. But when we do, we will be refreshed, renewed, rejuvenated, cleansed, and restored to a youthful joyous experience with the Lord. The scars of time and spiritual attacks will be washed away and left in the distant past. All things will be renewed and we will be enabled to fully let go of all hurts and bitterness. We will be transported far beyond any feelings of un-forgiveness. Truly all things will be restored. Wow!

> *"Ho! Everyone who thirsts, Come to the waters; and you who have no money, Come, buy and eat. Yes, come, buy wine and milk without money and without price. Why do you spend money for what is not bread, and your wages for what does not satisfy? Listen carefully to Me, and eat what is good, and let your soul delight itself in abundance. Incline your ear, and come to Me. Hear, and your soul shall live; and I will make an everlasting covenant with you—the sure mercies of David."* (Isaiah 55:1-3)

Then another revelation came. That water is available to you and me today. What are we waiting for? Let's draw from the well and drink deeply of this awesome gift of living water. Amen? *"Jesus answered her, "If you knew the gift of God and who it is that asks you for a drink, you would have asked him and he would have given you living water."* (John 4:10, NIV) There you have it! Jesus said that all you have to do is ask!

DAY 3

A TIME OF RESTORATION

T his morning, I had a lengthy time of praise and worship
followed by an awesome Third Heaven encounter. What
I was shown in this vision was truly awesome. I saw the glory
of God descend like a consuming fire onto a mountaintop. The
mountain was aglow with the fire and glory of God. Suddenly,
something like fire shot forth from the mountain toward me.
It spread out so that radiant beams of amber colored light
streaked in my direction. The beams of light were filled with
tiny glowing stars.

In the midst of this awesome display of God's glory, a very
large, heavily bejeweled crown made of blazing gold was sent
forth from the mountain. As it came closer, I could see that
the beauty of it was amazing, and I knew that no man was
worthy of this crown. As I continued to stand in this radiant
display of God's glory, I asked the Holy Spirit to reveal the
meaning of this vision. This is a summary of what the Holy
Spirit taught me:

We are entering a new season in the spiritual realm. This
is the season of the full restoration of the five-fold offices of
ministry. We have been experiencing this spiritual outpouring
in part, but God is now establishing it in fullness for the end
time preparation of the bride of Christ. This new season will
begin with the restoration of the apostolic office. This will be
followed by the restoration of each of the other four offices.
The apostolic must come first to provide the spiritual oversight
and structure for the other four. The crown represented a great
release of authority and a significant elevation in anointing. This

will usher in a season which will greatly challenge most people. Great spiritual insight will be needed to respond appropriately.

Then I saw people receiving other crowns. Some immediately fell down and cast their crowns at the feet of Jesus. Others put the crowns on their heads and stood very straight and appeared to be filled with pride. The Spirit said, "It is very important in this season to know who the real apostles are and which are false. This is how you will recognize the true apostles. They will not presume to wear the crowns. Instead, in true humility and complete submission to Christ they will fall at the feet of Jesus and give the crowns to the only one worthy to wear them (Jesus the Messiah). The false apostles will try to advance themselves claiming crowns that are not really for them. This is how you will know the true from the presumptive."

> *"Whenever the living creatures give glory, honor and thanks to him who sits on the throne and who lives for ever and ever, the twenty-four elders fall down before him who sits on the throne, and worship him who lives for ever and ever. They lay their crowns before the throne and say: "You are worthy, our Lord and God, to receive glory and honor and power, for you created all things, and by your will they were created and have their being."* (Revelation 4:9-11, NIV)

I believe that God is releasing this revelation to help us prepare ourselves to accept the authority of those God is placing in the apostolic offices. We must not respond with resistance and rebellion as the people did with Moses, the prophets, and Jesus himself. This will require us to be spiritually mature and fully submissive to the leading of the Holy Spirit. I daily pray in accordance with James 4:7-10 (NIV):

"Submit yourselves, then, to God. Resist the devil, and he will flee from you. Come near to God and he will come near to you. Wash your hands, you sinners, and purify your hearts, you double–minded. Grieve, mourn and wail. Change your laughter to mourning and your joy to gloom. Humble yourselves before the Lord, and he will lift you up."

This requires great wisdom on the part of the saints of God. I pray that God will give you wisdom and revelation for this season.

DAY 4

A BREAKER ANOINTING

In worship this morning, I kept hearing the Lord say, "I will inhabit your praise!" "I will inhabit your praise!" "I will inhabit your praise!" I was immediately reminded of people I meet periodically who always go over a list of all the things wrong in their lives. Along the way, they keep asking, "Where is the Lord in all this?" I heard the Lord say, "I did not say I will inhabit your complaints!"

I was reminded of the many people I meet who are struggling with their doubts. They will tell you all about them each time you meet. And during the litany of doubts, they ask, "Where is the Lord in all this?" Then I heard the Lord say, "I did not say I will inhabit your doubts!"

Many people I meet are struggling with fear and disillusionment. They tell me all about their problems which have led to these feelings. And during the litany of fears and disillusionment, they ask, "Where is the Lord in all this?" Then I heard the Lord, "I did not say I will inhabit your fears and disillusionment!"

If you are struggling with any of these emotions, remember what God is saying, "I will inhabit your praise!" Are you going through really rough times when provision, comfort and protection seem far away? Then praise the Lord who is your source of supply. Are you struggling with doubt and disillusionment? Then praise the Lord who sends grace and faith to meet every need. *"The breaker goes up before them; they break out, pass through the gate and go out by it. So their king goes on before them, and the Lord at their head."* (Micah 2:13, NASB)

I pray this breaker anointing on you today. May God break off every spirit working to hinder you from receiving all the Lord is releasing to you! May God break off the difficulties, doubts, disillusionment, and despair that the enemy uses against the Lord's people! May God release you into a new anointing of praise – a new level of glory! May you continue to move from glory to glory!

> *"But we all, with unveiled face, beholding as in a mirror the glory of the Lord, are being transformed into the same image from glory to glory, just as by the Spirit of the Lord."*
> (2 Corinthians 3:18)

As you look into the mirror today, may you see a new level of glory reflected back to you as God lifts up His countenance on you and through you!

DAY 5

ALIGNMENT IN AUTHORITY

T his morning, I heard the Lord say, "Align yourself! Align yourself in the anointing!" I received a lengthy set of instructions; some for all of us and some just for me. I will summarize the message here. Now it is your turn to go to the Holy Spirit to confirm and expand on this message. Remember who your helper is and call upon Him as you study. *"But the Helper, the Holy Spirit, whom the Father will send in My name, He will teach you all things, and bring to your remembrance all things that I said to you."* (John 14:26)

The Lord is saying that we have entered into a season when it is more critical than ever to be properly aligned with the flow of His Spirit. He has established an order for this outpouring. God is God, Jesus is Lord, and the Holy Spirit is our teacher, counselor, and guide. We must begin by understanding His order of authority, leadership, mentoring, and supply. We must all understand that this line of authority then branches out in an orderly manner through the 5-fold offices of ministry. This latter part is where we have difficulty, usually because of pride.

> *"And He Himself gave some to be apostles, some prophets, some evangelists, and some pastors and teachers, for the equipping of the saints for the work of ministry, for the edifying of the body of Christ, till we all come to the unity of the faith and of the knowledge of the Son of God, to a perfect man, to the measure of the stature of the fullness of Christ;"* (Ephesians 4:11-13)

In this proper alignment of His authority, we are built up and prepared for service in order to be mature and attain the full measure Christ has for us. The Lord told me that we must seek and know who is providing our apostolic covering (even if we are in that office for others). For the anointing to flow in our lives we must not jump from covering to covering looking for something that feels good or excites our mental processes. Proper apostolic covering will include guidance, teaching and mentoring. But, it will also include correction and occasional admonishment. We must not abandon the relationship when these realities are experienced. Improper alignment will hinder the flow of your anointing.

We need to know who the Lord is using to bring prophetic words to us, and stop jumping from prophet to prophet seeking more pleasant words of praise. Not all prophetic messages will be praise. Words that build-up, encourage and comfort may also present a challenge to move to a higher level of glory. We need to know who is in pastoral authority over us, and properly align with that authority to avoid hindering the flow of the impartation of grace. Pastors need pastors, teachers need teachers, prophets need prophetic words, and apostles need apostolic covering.

God is ready to release so much in the spirit realm because the time for preparing the bride of Christ is far spent. The release is being hindered by those of us who are out of alignment with the flow. Seek guidance from the Holy Spirit! Re-align yourself as soon as possible. Open your spirit to receive fresh oil of anointing, and new wine of provision.

> *"For I long to see you, that I may impart to you some spiritual gift, so that you may be established—that is, that I may be encouraged together with you by the mutual faith both of you and me."* (Romans 1:11-12)

Paul had been enabled to offer this impartation under the proper alignment of his apostolic covering. May God bless you through the Holy Spirit to move into the alignment He has established for you!

DAY 6

WALKING WITH THE LORD

This morning, as I worshipped the Lord, I asked Him the following questions. What can we do for you today, Lord? What would please you most today, Lord? Is there something we could do that would bless you today? What do you desire most from us today, Father? What can we do today to bring glory to your name!

I heard the Lord say, "The desire of my heart is to have fellowship with my children. I look at their day planners, and they are so busy. There is no space left for me. They are too busy to spend time with me. I have revealed my heart's desire over and over in my Word." Verses that reveal this began to flow in my mind. Through these verses, the Lord reminded me that he enjoyed walking, talking and visiting Adam and Eve in the cool of the day when it would be comfortable for them. *"And they heard the sound of the Lord God walking in the garden in the cool of the day,"* (Genesis 3:8a) Enoch walked so closely with the Lord that one day he just crossed over into Heaven. Moses talked with the Lord as a friend and Joshua always stayed close to the Tabernacle. Study the two passages below and claim these relationships with the Lord for yourself.

> *"Enoch lived sixty-five years, and begot Methuselah. After he begot Methuselah, Enoch walked with God three hundred years, and had sons and daughters. So all the days of Enoch were three hundred and sixty-five years. And Enoch walked with God; and he was not, for God took him."* (Genesis 5:21-24)

"So the Lord spoke to Moses face to face, as a man speaks to his friend. And he would return to the camp, but his servant Joshua the son of Nun, a young man, did not depart from the tabernacle." (Exodus 33:11)

The Lord said, "This is the pattern I set. This is my desire: to walk and talk with my children as Jesus walked and talked with two disciples on the road to Emmaus." Luke 24:13-15, *"Now behold, two of them were traveling that same day to a village called Emmaus, which was seven miles from Jerusalem. And they talked together of all these things which had happened. So it was, while they conversed and reasoned, that Jesus Himself drew near and went with them."* Then the Lord said, "Most of my children are afraid of this level of intimacy with me."

When Adam and Eve were afraid and ashamed they avoided the walk with God and tried to hide from Him. When God invited the people to come up on the mountain with Moses for a face to face visit, they were too afraid to go. I remind you that God is in a good mood. He doesn't want to harm you. He wants to bless you, give you purpose, give you vision, and give you hope.

I know that my heart's desire is to walk and talk with the Lord today and every day. How about you? As busy as he is, He is available for you? As full as His day planner may ever get, He has time set aside for you. It is His heart's desire to spend time with you today. The door to the secret place is open. Come on in and sit with the Lord for a little while! He has planted a garden. Come, walk, and talk with Him in the cool of the day! May you walk in intimate fellowship with the Lord today!

DAY 7

IN HIS PRESENCE

W e were awake until well after midnight following a long night of worship and ministry. At 4:55 a.m. the Lord awakened me so I could spend time with Him. As I got out of bed, the face of the clock changed to 4:56 a.m., and it came to me that there was something significant about this time. So, I checked out Isaiah 45 verses 5 and 6: "*I am the Lord, and there is no other; there is no God besides Me. I will gird you, though you have not known Me, that they may know from the rising of the sun to its setting that there is none besides Me. I am the Lord, and there is no other;*" (Isaiah 45:5-6)

As I moved into the Lord's presence, I saw an open heaven. As I looked intently into that opening, a huge cluster of grapes appeared, and I pressed in to get to the grapes. As we entered (I was very conscious of not being alone – you were with me), I was fascinated by this huge bunch of grapes. They looked like they were made of pure gold. I waited to see if I would be offered a taste. As I waited a table appeared, and it was surrounded by what looked like wrought iron chairs for a poolside or patio setting. However, they were made of pure gold instead of painted iron. Thick plush cushions were on each chair.

As we were invited to take our places around the table, I was reminded that many churches celebrate the Lord's Supper on the first Sunday and this was beginning to look like a communion service. As we each took our place around the table, the Lord appeared. I noticed that we each now had a cup from the cluster of grapes, but there was no bread on the table. As this thought went through my mind, the Lord answered. He said, "I am the bread!" When He said this, His body was transfigured as on the mountaintop with His disciples. In the intense brightness of His presence, beams of light shot out from His body into each of us and we received of the true spiritual bread of heaven. Then we all knew that we were to drink of the cup.

No words were spoken, but it was as if we each received a deeper revelation of the meaning of redemption than we had ever known before. We just suddenly knew that it was not about accepting Jesus to escape hell. It was about entering into a deep personal relationship with Him. There was no thought of avoiding something. There was only this passionate love drawing us ever closer to Him. It wasn't about obeying a set of rules (do's and don'ts). It was about His presence being all in all. It had nothing to do with how much we had done or how much we deserved it. It was about the garment of His righteousness which was now covering each of us.

I realized that I knew these things intellectually as you know them. But, suddenly, I knew it and you knew it at a revelatory level deeper than anything we had known before. It wasn't about how much we knew about the Bible and about Him. It was about how much He knew about us and we were there anyway. An awesome sense of gratitude (the most pure thanksgiving we had ever given – without words – just in the spirit) filled all of us beyond anything we thought possible.

I felt so thrilled by the revelation knowledge that there is so much more to understand and accept about the redemption he won for us at Calvary. It was so exciting to understand that we will still be learning and getting excited about it 10,000 years from now – and for all eternity. Wow! What an exciting future in store for each of us who are passionately in love with Jesus and through Him passionate lovers of our Father God.

May you experience a deeper sense of His presence today than you have ever experienced before in your entire lifetime! And, may tomorrow bring so much more that what you have today will only seem like the beginning! May each and every day bring more and more of His presence into your life, family and ministry! May you begin to really know that you know that you know that He is all in all! May you be totally consumed by gratitude and thanksgiving both now and forever! Can you feel that? Can you feel His presence right now! I hope and pray that you are being overwhelmed by Him right now. What I am feeling right now is awesome, and I want more for you! Amen!!!

———————————

DAY 8

MAKE TIME FOR HIM

T his morning, I had an extended visit in heaven with the Lord and received loads of instructions including three sermons to preach in the near future. I asked the Lord to tell me what to share this morning. He said, "I want to spend time with each of you this week. Check your Monday motives. Are you more concerned with all the tasks you have to do this week than with setting aside time to spend with me?"

> *"Therefore do not worry, saying, 'What shall we eat?' or 'What shall we drink?' or 'What shall we wear?' For after all these things the Gentiles seek. For your heavenly Father knows that you need all these things. But seek first the kingdom of God and His righteousness, and all these things shall be added to you. Therefore do not worry about tomorrow, for tomorrow will worry about its own things. Sufficient for the day is its own trouble."* (Matthew 6:31-34)

It is so easy to get caught up in activities and plans while forgetting the most important things. Earlier, I had gone through a long list of things I had to do this week: mow the lawn before the Home Owners Association gets upset; get connected with the people who are building our storage building; set up a time for the construction of the fence, and etc. So, I had to break all that stuff off in order to have a time of intimacy with the Lord. Actually, I had to break it off several times before I could really move into His presence.

Being with the Lord is such an awesome experience! How could we ever let anything take away that precious time? I pray that we will all cultivate that desire in our hearts to spend time with Him. I pray that you will have awesome times of soaking in His presence while He builds you up in your most holy faith. I pray that He will impart greater grace and greater glory into your heart today and each day. I pray that you will feel His love and know His goodness in your life, your work, your ministry, and in your family. Amen!

DAY 9

OBEDIENCE IS THE KEY

As always, I prayed this morning for the Holy Spirit to tell me what heaven is saying today. Jesus promised that the Holy Spirit would guide us into all truth and based on that promise I asked to know the truth about what would please the Father today. Immediately, I heard, "Obedience!" I paused to hear more, and the Lord said, "It is the same as it has always been. Obedience pleases Father God."

> *"But Samuel replied: "Does the LORD delight in burnt offerings and sacrifices as much as in obeying the voice of the LORD? To obey is better than sacrifice, and to heed is better than the fat of rams."* (1 Samuel 15:22, NIV)

When Jesus gave us the Great Commission, He said, *"teaching them to observe all things that I have commanded you;"* (Matthew 28:20a) Teaching what Jesus commanded is something we have not always done well. In fact, I have asked many people in ministry what Jesus commanded, and few have ever answered beyond love of God and neighbor. However, Jesus commanded many things as recorded in the four gospels (i.e. *"Heal the sick, cleanse the lepers, raise the dead, cast out demons. Freely you have received, freely give."* – Matthew 10:8)

Peter says that the Holy Spirit is given to those who obey. *"And we are His witnesses to these things, and so also is the Holy Spirit whom God has given to those who obey Him."* (Acts 5:32) If we desire to operate in the gifts and power of the Holy Spirit, we must be obedient to the commands of the Lord.

Virtually all of God's promises are connected to obedience. John connects answered prayer to obedience and then makes it clear that we are not in Him, or He in us unless we obey His commands.

> *"Dear friends, if our hearts do not condemn us, we have confidence before God and receive from him anything we ask, because we obey his commands and do what pleases him. And this is his command: to believe in the name of his Son, Jesus Christ, and to love one another as he commanded us. Those who obey his commands live in him, and he in them. And this is how we know that he lives in us: We know it by the Spirit he gave us."* (1 John 3:21-24, NIV)

We have taught freedom from "the Law" so zealously, that an entire generation has believed that obedience is somewhat optional, and God will love us and bless us whether we obey or not. This is not a Biblical concept. It is true that we do not win our salvation through obedience or good works. However, if we want to stay in the blessing flow – if we want the prayer of faith to be answered – if we want to move in the gifts of the Spirit – if we want the favor of God, we must live in obedience to the commands of Christ.

With all of my spirit, soul, and body, I want to be a student (disciple) of Jesus Christ. I want to know what He commanded. I want to teach it to His modern day disciples. I want to live a life that is pleasing to the Father, the Son, and the Holy Spirit. And, I want to live in a way that will not grieve the Holy Spirit. This morning, the Holy Spirit was reminding me that all these things are tied to obedience.

As a teenager, I thought all the commands were given to prevent us from having fun and living life to the full. I am no longer a teenager. During my 67 years of life, I have found that I am in the blessing flow (God's unmerited grace – favor) when I am living in obedience. I have found that joy, peace, prosperity, blessing, grace, power, authority, and every other gift are most strongly present when I am in obedience. Real happiness is found in Him and as John said, we are in Him when we obey. For me, this was a very good word today. As for me, I love to hear this word from heaven.

May you know the intense pleasure of the presence of the Lord in your life today and always! May you have the peace that passes understanding as you live in unity with Him as obedient disciples! May you have all the confidence and assurance which comes to those who trust and obey! May you be prepared and ready for His return! Amen!!!

DAY 10

BEING SPIRIT LED

This morning, the Lord gave me an open vision of a railroad crossing. The lights were flashing, the bells were ringing, and the red and white striped arms were coming down to block the crossing. I heard the Lord say, "This is a time to pause and wait for something powerful from the enemy to pass harmlessly by you. He often comes at you from the left side (opposite of side of authority) and attempts to run over you with destructive power. Listen to the warnings you receive from the Holy Spirit. Go when He says go, and stop when He says stop. He will alert you and protect you from the attacks of the enemy."

How many people have refused to listen to the guidance given by the Holy Spirit and made a train wreck of their lives and ministries? While in the body, Jesus himself operated under the guidance of the Spirit: *"Then Jesus, being filled with the Holy Spirit, returned from the Jordan and was led by the Spirit into the wilderness, being tempted for forty days by the devil."* (Luke 4:1-2a)

And, Jesus promised, *"However, when He, the Spirit of truth, has come, He will guide you into all truth; for He will not speak on His own authority, but whatever He hears He will speak; and He will tell you things to come."* (John 16:13) I know that you know these things. I believe the message this morning was not so much a new message as a call to live by the Word which has already been given. Operate in the gifts of the Spirit which have already been released, and press in for more of each gift. The enemy is always up to something.

He isn't very creative. He uses the same tactics over and over, and God's people seem surprised each time.

Peter from his own experience warned us: "*Dear friends, do not be surprised at the painful trial you are suffering, as though something strange were happening to you.*" (1 Peter 4:12, NIV) Peter reminds us that the same attacks came against Jesus and all His followers. Don't be surprised! Expect it, and let the Spirit lead you safely through it. Like the apostles in the book of Acts, we need to learn to follow the Spirit. Go where He leads, and stop when He says, "Stop!" "*So, being sent out by the Holy Spirit, they went down to Seleucia, and from there they sailed to Cyprus.*" (Acts 13:4)

People who claim to be "Spirit led" need to honor the Holy Spirit by following His leadership. "*Now when they had gone through Phrygia and the region of Galatia, they were forbidden by the Holy Spirit to preach the word in Asia.*" (Acts 16:6) This morning, I was assured again that the Holy Spirit will lead us to the place of God's anointing and to the greatest harvest. From time to time, I need these reminders. Perhaps you need them, too. Remember, the Holy Spirit will protect you from the moves of the enemy.

The Lord was saying this morning that He is releasing a greater anointing for discernment of enemy plans and movements. If you will receive this gift and operate in it, God will guide, provide, protect, and prosper you, your family, and your ministry. May you clearly hear the guidance of the Holy Spirit! May you increase in the spiritual gift of discernment! May you clearly see the movement and guidance of the Holy Spirit! May your spiritual eyes and ears be opened more and more to discern what the enemy is bringing against you before it happens! May you walk in the wisdom and might of the Holy Spirit today and always! Amen!

DAY 11

SURPRISED BY THE LORD

During my worship time this morning, I felt the presence of the Lord so strongly that I began to walk around our worship room with my hands lifted to the Lord and singing His praise. At one point, it felt as if I stepped on a very wet place on the carpet. I looked back at that spot but didn't see any water. The next time around, I stepped into something wet again. I looked at the ceiling to see if there was a leak from the roof. No! Then I wondered if a pipe had broken under the carpet. No! Everything was normal in appearance on the floor.

The next time around, I felt it again, but then something changed. As I continued to walk and praise the Lord, it was wet all the way around the room. Then I began to sense that I was walking through water about one inch deep – then two inches deep – and then three inches deep. At this point, my attention was directed to the music I was singing. I had been walking around the room singing, "Rise up within me living water — Spirit of God in me! Holy Spirit guide me! Saturate my Soul!"

I was so overcome by gratitude and praise that I went face down on the carpet and gave Him praise and thanksgiving with joy in my heart. In my spirit I was lifted to the Throne Room with the Father and the Son as I continued to praise and worship. I asked the Holy Spirit to teach me what Heaven is saying today. I prayed to know what would please the Father today. I asked for a message from heaven for you. Then the Holy Spirit told me that what really pleases the Father is to bless His children. The Spirit taught me that the Father loves to give living water to His children and to let them feel His loving presence.

Then I heard the Holy Spirit say, "The Father loves to surprise His children. He loves to do something that surprises you and catches you off guard so that He can pour out more. What you can do for the Father today is to be open to receive it. Be open for a wonderful surprise as He pours out blessings into you. Keep your spiritual eyes and ears open to what the Father will pour out to you today!" The spiritual water on the carpet certainly did that for me this morning. A scripture very special to me kept going through my mind. *"Every good gift and every perfect gift is from above, and comes down from the Father of lights, with whom there is no variation or shadow of turning."* (James 1:17)

After coming downstairs to my office, I looked up this verse and read it over a few times. Then I noticed the next verse, James 1:18, *"Of His own will He brought us forth by the word of truth, that we might be a kind of firstfruits of His creatures."* All of this pouring out is for the purpose of bringing us forth by the word of truth so we can become the first-fruits of His new creation. Again my heart was filled with gratitude. The plans and purposes of the Father are so awesome and wonderful beyond all we can ask or imagine.

Step into the water today! Let Him saturate your soul! Let the living waters rise up within you! Be filled with the Spirit and walk with your spiritual eyes and ears open. The "Father of lights" has good and perfect gifts for you today. Remember there is no shadow of turning or variation in Him. What He has promised, He will fulfill.

May you feel His powerful presence today! May you be soaked in living water and saturated with the Holy Spirit! May you be open and receive all the gifts He has for you today and always! Amen!!!!

DAY 12

STRENGTH FROM LOVE

This morning, I asked the Holy Spirit to guide me in understanding the truth as promised by Jesus. I asked to hear what heaven is saying today. This is what I received: "If you want power, praise more! If you want power gifts, love more! Do not be like those Paul foresaw: *"having a form of godliness but denying its power. And from such people turn away!"* (2 Timothy 3:5) You are not to be powerless. God did not give you a spirit of power to make you meek and weak. Look at 2 Timothy 1:7 (NIV), *"For God did not give us a spirit of timidity, but a spirit of power, of love and of self-discipline."* Those who witness powerfully must witness in power."

I was given a vision of a tree standing tall and strong with the glory of the Lord surrounding it with such brightness that it appeared almost as a silhouette. At first, I thought the tree was in heaven because of the brilliance of the glory around it. However, I was shown that it was on the earth. The winds blew, and the tree was completely unaffected. It did not sway in the wind nor was even one leaf moved by the flow of natural air. An earthquake came, and again the tree was unaffected. The Lord said, "The tree is a witness to the power and presence of God. You are a witness for the Lord! Stand tall and strong! Do not be afraid or affected by the powers of this world."

The Holy Spirit guided me through a meditation on this word from heaven. "You can only receive power when you are connected continuously with the Lord in your praise and worship. So, if you want power, praise more. God can only trust you with as many power gifts as your love can handle. If you have power without love, you will do harm to yourself and others. Power without love will be a witness against what the Father is trying to do through your life and ministry. *"Pursue love, and desire spiritual gifts, but especially that you may prophesy."* (1 Corinthians 14:1) Power comes when your primary pursuit is love.

The body of Christ has been weak and meek too long. It is time to demonstrate again the power of God. This power will be released through those called to serve Him in the great end-time harvest. The world is so filled with unbelief! The enemy has veiled the eyes of the church and led them into false doctrine. It is time to go back to the gospel of the kingdom and be obedient to Christ. An unbelieving world will not be swayed by a weak and meek group embracing poverty, sickness, and powerlessness.

Without the power of God, you cannot be obedient to Christ's command: *"Heal the sick, cleanse the lepers, raise the dead, cast out demons. Freely you have received, freely give."* (Matthew 10:8) You can't do the first until you have received the latter part of this command. The Father wants you to freely receive. You cannot give away what you don't have. What will please the Father today (and always) is for us to be obedient and *"Pursue love, and desire spiritual gifts, but especially that you may prophesy."* Jesus said: *"Ask, and it will be given to you; seek, and you will find; knock, and it will be opened to you. For everyone who asks receives, and he who seeks finds, and to him who knocks it will be opened. Or what man is there among you who, if his son asks for bread, will give him a stone? Or if he asks for a fish, will he give him a serpent? If you then, being evil, know how to give good gifts to your children, how much more will your Father who is in heaven give good things to those who ask Him!"* (Matthew 7:7-11)

May the Lord fill you with a desire to pursue love in order to equip you for the power Jesus promised! May you desire earnestly and intensely to receive the gifts of the Spirit to empower you for greater service in His kingdom! May you receive freely so that you are inspired to freely give! May the Lord impart spiritual power into your life and ministry in greater measure than you have ever asked or imagined! May you be fully equipped for proclaiming the gospel of the kingdom! Amen!

DAY 13

JOY REPLACES HEAVINESS

I approached my time of worship this morning with a spirit of heaviness over me. I spent extra time in worship and praise as I marched around the room giving thanksgiving and praise to Father God. The Lord sent me back downstairs to get my shofar and rams horn. I then began to spiritually march around Jericho blowing the shofar and rams horn to bring down the walls of the enemy fortification.

When the heaviness lifted, I went face down on the floor in submission to God. I recommitted myself to His purposes and His plans. Then I asked to hear what heaven is saying today. Suddenly, I had a beautiful vision of the open heavens. The glory of the Lord was bursting forth in abundance. I heard the Lord saying, "For those who enter my Sabbath rest, I will pour out my glory; my goodness; and my grace in abundance today. I spent some time just receiving that and being thankful. I thought that this might be all I would receive today, and it was certainly enough. However, I wanted more. I rolled over on my back.

As I rolled over, an amazing vision was given. I saw huge windows of various shapes and sizes passing overhead. Then open Bibles which were glowing with some sort of internal light began to float overhead. I began to reach up and take the Bibles. I grasped one and placed it on my forehead and waited for it to sink in. Then I grasped another one and placed it over my heart and waited for it to sink in. I remembered the story of the king being told to strike the ground with arrows and stopping after the third time. The prophet then said that he made a big mistake and would only have limited success. I didn't want that to happen to me so I just continued to grasp the word and bring it down into my spirit, soul and body. Then I heard the Lord say, "You chose well. It is vital to have wisdom and revelation from my Word before you try to bring things down from the open heaven. Without wisdom, you will be tempted to obtain the wrong gifts for your ministry and calling."

Other things began to pour forth from the windows. I saw hearts floating where the Bibles had been before. I began to reach up and pull down those hearts and press them into my heart and mind. The Lord reminded me of Paul's teaching to pursue love before desiring spiritual gifts. My sincere desire is to have the heart of Jesus: to love who He loves; to love what He loves; and to bless as He blesses. I felt very much strengthened by the Word and the love I had taken into my heart and mind. Then I began to see something like little clear globes floating above. They all contained spiritual gifts. With wisdom, revelation, and love, I began to select the gifts and bring them down. This time I added something. I pressed them into my belly. I want rivers of living water to flow forth from my belly as Jesus promised.

This may sound strange to you, but I believe this is one of the ways we ask, seek, and knock to make the gifts of the spirit real in our lives. We can't just sit passively watching things go by. We need to reach out and grasp the things of the Spirit. I wanted all I could get from this open heaven and I continue to bring down everything I could get my hands on. I saw financial resources for ministry, and reached out for them placing them in my pockets until they were filled. I knew that without financial resources being released, we were going to have difficulty responding to God's plan for our ministry. So, I took all that was offered.

This was a wonderful experience! However, I knew that something was missing. I just wasn't aware of what the missing ingredient might be. Then I saw something different coming out of the windows of heaven. It looked like a Christmas ornament with bright colors and ribbons stretching forth beyond the globe that contained it. I looked intently at it, and saw the word, "JOY!" I grasped that one with both hands and pressed it into my spirit. As I pressed it in, I was aware that the heaviness was gone; replaced by the joy of the Lord. Wow! What a wonderful morning! I traded all my worthless heaviness for these precious gifts from heaven.

I pray that you will see an open heaven today and reach out to grasp every spiritual gift you need. Remember to get the Word first and the wisdom and revelation it brings. Don't stop until you are fully loaded (filled) with the wisdom of God! Then in that wisdom and in accordance with the Word, reach up and take what you need for your life and ministry. Please remember to take the joy of the Lord. It makes all the other gifts flow and function better and better.

We are in a time of preparation and resourcing for the next mighty move of God. He is giving what we need in order to be equipped in this new season. May you receive more than you ask or imagine. There are no limits when heaven is open. Grasp what you need in the spirit and trust in faith that these will soon manifest in the natural. AMEN!

BE STILL IN HIS PRESENCE

T his morning as I worshipped the Lord, there was an awesome outpouring of His presence. I saw words written in blue in arch shaped formations being released from heaven. I couldn't read these words because they were in a language unfamiliar to me. I prayed for understanding and experienced another great flow of the joy of the Lord. That was wonderful, and I wanted more. So, I prayed in the spirit for a long time. As I prayed, I was caught up into heaven. I moved through a large portal and was placed on a mountaintop overlooking a beautiful mountain range.

It was like early morning with clouds hanging so low that they appeared to be fog flowing like water through all the valleys before me. It was a beautiful sight. I learned to love this kind of scene flying in helicopters over the mountain ranges of Korea. As I enjoyed these scenes, I came to a deeper realization that all the things we love are present in heaven. Then I heard His voice. He said, "Be still and know that I am God!" My thoughts went to Psalm 46:10, *"Be still, and know that I am God; I will be exalted among the nations, I will be exalted in the earth!"*

I thought, "I am being very still! I'm on the floor face down before the Lord. I am still!" Then I heard the Lord say, "No! You are not really still." I began to notice that my body can't be still no matter how hard I try. My heart keeps beating. My lungs keep breathing. I can't really be still. So, this must not be what the Lord is talking about. My heart (my spirit) was in such peace on this beautiful mountain and it seemed very still in the presence of God, but then the joy of the Lord came. How can my heart be still in His presence? It can't. So, what does this mean?

Then the Holy Spirit revealed my problem. It's my mind. I wasn't keeping my mind still. I began to pray in the spirit because I know that my mind is still while I am doing that. It worked! After I stopped praying in the spirit, my mind was still for a little while. Then it started moving again. So, I went back to praying in the spirit. My mind was still, and I began to get an awesome revelation of God being God. Of course at that very moment, my mind started racing with thoughts about that. So, I lost the stillness again and the deep revelation of who He is began to fade. I did it over again, and got it back for a little while. I had to do this over and over just to hold on to it for a short while.

Then the Holy Spirit began to reveal some truth to me in response to my daily prayer to be guided into all the truth I can handle. We are not good at keeping our minds still and this is one of the main reasons we don't know more of who God is. We are so busy telling Him who He is that we don't stop, get still, and let Him tell us who He is. The Spirit gave me another verse, *"Meditate within your heart on your bed, and be still."* (Psalm 4:4b) This is something we are supposed to practice. Being still only comes with time and practice. We are always so busy. We have grown up in societies that measure value by products produced through activity and work. We have not learned to value being still. Yet, this is the way that we come to know Him better. What shall we do?

When I heard the Lord's voice this morning saying, "Be still and know that I am God," it didn't have the tone of a suggestion. It was a command. I know that I must do this more. Practice improves any skill. This is part of the meat of the Word. Remember: *"But solid food belongs to those who are of full age, that is, those who by reason of use have their senses exercised to discern both good and evil."* (Hebrews 5:14) Spiritual senses and spiritual gifts are increased through use – practice, practice, practice.

Are you practicing His presence? Can you be still so that He can reveal Himself to you? I am not very good at it, but I am getting better. I am getting better because I have been taught to practice it. May you learn to be still in your mind and receive a deeper and deeper understanding of who God is! Remember, He said, "Be still and know that I am God!" Amen?

P.S. I believe this is what was written in blue letters and being released from heaven at the beginning of this time with the Lord. The Father is trying so hard to make Himself known to His people. He wants you to hear from Him and know who He is. He isn't hiding. It is His desire to reveal more and more of Himself to you.

DAY 15

STANDING STRONG

This morning, the Lord gave me a very surprising vision as the Holy Spirit guided me through some truth. In the vision, I was standing in what appeared to be the only chamber in a large cave. Against the back wall, I saw a very large circular stone covered with some type of ancient writing. Time had not been kind to the message carved into this old sandstone wheel. So much erosion had occurred that it was almost impossible to decipher the writing. The stone had split into two pieces with one piece being 2/3 of the whole. Suddenly the large piece rolled back by some invisible force opening a passage beyond the entrance chamber. I knew that I was entering the secret place as I moved into the next level of the cave.

As I passed through the stone door and looked around, I realized that I was in the catacombs of an ancient city, and I had entered an ancient burial room. It was very musty and dusty. As the stone rolled back a very rare breeze was allowed to flow into the cave. This breeze caused very old fragments of burial clothes and drapes over chambers to move with the flow of air. I felt that I had entered a sacred place and was unsure if I should be in a place like this. Then I noticed a faint glow of light coming from much deeper in the cave. I felt the presence of the Lord and the light appeared as His glory flowing forth from something occurring deep in the cave. I moved toward the light and felt myself being drawn near a place of deep and reverent worship of the Lord. I was unsure about proceeding further, but I was drawn to move into some ancient fellowship and give the praise, honor, and glory our Lord so richly deserves.

I asked the Holy Spirit to give me understanding, and He was faithful to guide me into His truth. I heard Him saying, "In times of persecution, the church is at its best. Only the true worshippers will endure such hardships to worship and serve when they risk the loss of business, family, and life. Only those who truly love the Lord wholeheartedly will venture to a place like this to honor and bless their Father God. How many in your time would still worship under these threats or in a place like this? As long as it is very comfortable, entertaining, and non-committal people will come. But, as soon as a challenge comes or things become difficult or dangerous, they fall away. Meditate on this! Would you come to a place like this to worship?"

Wow! That was heavy. I was humbled. I felt such a deep respect for those in times past who have stayed committed under conditions like this. I knew the answers to the Spirit's questions, but I didn't want to acknowledge them. I have seen it over and over – a little conflict or mild criticism and people leave and never return. People flee when their relationship with the Lord requires sacrifice or suffering. I felt a deep desire to be like those who were worshipping in the catacombs, but was confronted with the question, "Would you?" How much tribulation will the Lord's sheep tolerate before they scatter, hide, or even deny their Lord? We know what happened to the disciples when it suddenly came upon them. What about you and me?

Thank God! He is so faithful and good! When we have scattered in fear or failure, He always welcomes us back. He puts trust in people who have already demonstrated that they can't be trusted. He restores those who don't deserve it. Thank God for His faithfulness! May God bless you to grow into a higher level of faithfulness and commitment! May the Lord set you free from the fear of man so you can be totally dedicated to Him! I pray for boldness to proclaim the gospel of the kingdom and to lift up the name of Jesus no matter what the cost may be! I pray that we will have an Acts 4 experience of the outpouring of the Holy Spirit in answer to our prayers! Amen!

DAY 16

AN OCEAN OF LOVE

As I went before the Lord this morning, I went into an open vision and found myself on a beach near the ocean. However, what I saw in this vision was very unusual. My view of the horizon was vertical instead of horizontal. As I meditated on that, I began to realize that it was as if I was on my right side looking at the scene, but I was standing up. Somehow I was horizontal in this vision which made the scene look vertical. I heard the Lord say, "The ocean you are seeing is a symbol of my love. There is more than enough to wash, cleanse, purify, and empower everyone who has ever lived or ever will live. When you try to see it from your perspective, you get a distorted view. When you try to see Me from your perspective you adjust what you see to meet your expectations."

I accepted this word and sought to see things from His perspective. The vision shifted so that the horizon was now horizontal, but now I only had a small circular view of a distant part of the ocean. The view was crystal clear in the center, but became more and more blurred toward the edges of the circle. I was seeing a very distant and small portion of the love of God. Then the Lord said to me, "My people have spiritual cataracts. Their peripheral vision is blocked and they only see my love as some distant reality. But, even this limited view inspires them to praise, write songs, and give thanksgiving. I want to remove their cataracts so they can see much, much more, but they have to be willing and seek it."

I prayed for the eyes of my heart to be opened so I could see more of God's love. Suddenly, my full vision was restored, and I saw powerful waves crashing into the rocky coastline in front of me. The power of the waves crashing against the stony shore was awesome and took my breath away with the suddenness of this experience. I was in awe in this expanded experience of the Love of God. His love was crashing against the rocky shore of my heart breaking down old strongholds and steadily wearing away the rocks of resistance. I was so filled with gratitude for this perspective of His love, that I was barely able to express my deep sense of thanksgiving.

The power of His love was wonderful, but at the same time the magnitude of it was frightening. With one wave, I could be wiped out and washed away, but He chose to free me, cleanse me, renew me, and bless me with all that power. Awesome! Father God is so good. I heard the Lord say, "That fear you felt is one of the reasons people have cataracts. They do not yet trust me enough to open their hearts to receive the full power of my love because they fear my judgments. If they could only understand what I really want to do in their lives, I could quickly heal their spiritual blindness."

I prayed for more healing, and the Lord showed me a succession of awe inspiring scenes from various places around the world. I saw sunrises over the ocean of His love. I saw sunsets over the ocean of His love. Each successive scene appeared more beautiful and awe inspiring than the one before. I was caught up in God's love. Filled with that love, I thought of you, and prayed that you too would have a grand revelation of His powerful and awe inspiring love. I prayed that the eyes of your heart would open wide as God blesses you with more and more of His love and grace. May you be filled, cleansed, restored and enlivened by His awesome love today and forever! Amen!

DAY 17

ARE YOU LISTENING?

This morning, I struggled with a wandering mind again. As I focused on thanksgiving, praise, and worship, I would gradually return to thoughts about the construction projects which will begin in a few days on our property. We are experiencing additional challenges to our plans caused by the building of a house next door. I caught my mind wandering again, and then refocused on praise and worship. After a long struggle, I finally had the breakthrough. Has that ever happened to you?

In that final breakthrough, the Lord gave me a vision of a giant ear appearing in the open heaven before me. I pondered the meaning, and then I heard the Lord say: "Are you listening to me? Immediately Ezekiel 12:2 came into my spirit, *"Son of man, you dwell in the midst of a rebellious house, which has eyes to see but does not see, and ears to hear but does not hear; for they are a rebellious house."* I don't want to be part of a rebellious house which has ears but chooses not to hear the Lord. The gospels record Jesus saying many times, *"He who has ears to hear, let him hear!"* How tragic to have the ability and still not hear Him.

As I meditated on these thoughts, a huge silver trumpet appeared next to the ear, and I heard the Lord saying, "Are you listening for this sound? Will you hear it when the last great trumpet sounds at the time of my return? Are you watching, waiting, and listening for me?" I reflected on the following two scriptures: 1. Matthew 24:42, *"Watch therefore, for you do not know what hour your Lord is coming."* and 2. Matthew

25:13, *"Watch therefore, for you know neither the day nor the hour in which the Son of Man is coming."*

This message was received a few days before the Feast of Trumpets. Trusting that the Lord will keep His timetable in the future as He has in the past, I am expecting to hear this trumpet during this feast sometime in the future. If it is this year, I want to hear it first. If it sounds any year during my lifetime, I want to be found watching, waiting, and listening for it. I want to be ready for His return. So, I took these words from the Lord to heart. I am more focused than ever on listening to hear His voice, to be watching for His return, and to be listening for the sound of that trumpet.

> *"Watch therefore, for you do not know when the master of the house is coming—in the evening, at midnight, at the crowing of the rooster, or in the morning—lest, coming suddenly, he find you sleeping. And what I say to you, I say to all: Watch!"* (Mark 13:35-37)

When the Lord returns, may he find you watching, waiting, and listening! May He find you about your Father's business! May He find you prepared in spirit, soul, and body fully ready to enter His kingdom to dwell with Him forever and ever! Amen!

A SECOND MESSAGE ON THE SAME DAY

In our Tuesday night "Soaking Service," I received a word from the Lord for all of those present. During worship, I was compelled to get face down on the floor. The Lord began to press on me to proclaim a call for those present to be intercessors and watchers over the region in which we live (from Columbia, South Carolina through Charlotte, North Carolina). The Lord told me to anoint those present with oil and commission them as watchers over this region.

While I lay on the floor, I went into an open vision in which I was high above Korea (similar to a view from a satellite). As I looked down on the Korean peninsula, I saw two powerful spiritual forces at war. I saw a huge battle between the powers of light and the powers of darkness. The Lord told me that Korea is a vital link in the release of the end time harvest. Because the Korean people are so hungry for the Lord and so willing to press in to receive every anointing and every impartation, God will honor that hunger by releasing a massive revival that will spread around the world.

Because the Lord's plan has been revealed, the enemy has responded with a massive attack on the church in Korea attempting to rob them of their spiritual destiny and delay the end time harvest. The Lord brought back to my memory the many people we have met from Korea in the last few months who have shared great spiritual struggles going on right now in their churches. We have talked to some since their return to Korea who have experienced stronger warfare than ever in the church. The enemy is seeking those who are spiritually weak to use them to bring rebellion and disharmony to the body of Christ. These individuals are not aware that they are being influenced by the enemy to block the body of Christ and prevent the church from reaching its God given destiny. I hear of people who are criticizing and attacking their pastors and their pastors' wives bringing disunity and struggles within their congregations.

As this was being revealed to me, I saw angels kneeling and praying above Korea. I heard a call for Korean believers around the world to join together in agreement to break the power of darkness and the enemy's attempts to stop the great army of the faithful which God has called forth. I heard a call for people who are willing to forgo their limited desires for their own congregations and join together to pray for the kingdom of God to come on earth as it is in heaven. I heard a call for those who could celebrate the advancement of the kingdom of God even if it didn't happen in their own churches – a call for people who are more kingdom focused than self-centered – people who can rejoice when the church across the street grows faster than their own church – people who celebrate the advancement of the kingdom of God wherever it happens.

I heard a call for those who are able to envision greater things for the nations; who can now think beyond anything they have ever imagined in the past. I heard the Lord calling for intercessory prayer warriors who are going after the nations because it is God's heart to win them all. I saw a huge circle of fire forming over Korea as God began to release this great revival. Shafts of light and fire were shooting forth from this circle and touching Korean people everywhere with the fire of revival. Korean people who have immigrated to various nations of the world were kindling the fires of revival coming from Korea in every nation of the world.

I shared with a group in one of our meetings about an experience we had at a church in Columbia a few weeks ago. The pastor asked the congregation, "How many churches are there in Columbia?" I wondered if they really knew because there are so many. The whole congregation answered correctly as one voice, saying, **ONE!** The pastor affirmed their answer. Jesus only has one church and we should be more concerned and committed to that church than our own small part in it. Wow! I was impressed by the insight of this pastor. He has been teaching this message for the last ten years, and they have all grasped this powerful truth. I was thankful for this experience, because it widened my perspective. The Lord called me to anoint those present in our service and commission them for this awesome calling. The Holy Spirit was powerfully present as we participated in this commissioning service.

This morning the Lord placed it on my heart to share this vision and call on all His people to receive this commissioning and begin to be coals of fire around the world to ignite revival fires in all nations. Are you one of the ones willing to be coals of fire for revival where God has placed you? If so, ask the Holy Spirit to release that anointing to you and join with us in a commitment to daily prayer for the release of God's power over your region and over the nation of Korea. What starts there will go around the world into every nation on earth. Even now, the fires are beginning to break out. I give thanks to our God and Father for what He is now doing! I give thanks to our Lord Jesus Christ who made it all possible! I give thanks be to the Holy Spirit who carries the fire and releases it through us. Amen!

PRESENCE OR PRESENTS

Today, I went before the Lord expecting to receive a message. For a very long time, I received nothing. I was face down before the Lord for all this time, but nothing came. I rolled over on my back for a long time, but nothing came. My heart cried out to the Lord as I wondered why Heaven was so silent on this day. Have you ever prayed like that? I rolled back over face down before the Lord, and then the Lord gave me understanding. Our motives in coming to Him are the key. The Lord was saying, "You must come before me desiring my presence instead of just desiring "presents." It matters more what you come to give than what you come to get. If you are only coming to Me to get something, it doesn't honor Me, bless Me or minister to Me." I remembered Jesus' words in Matthew Chapter six:

> *"Therefore do not worry, saying, 'What shall we eat?' or 'What shall we drink?' or 'What shall we wear?' For after all these things the Gentiles seek. For your heavenly Father knows that you need all these things. But seek first the kingdom of God and His righteousness, and all these things shall be added to you."* (Matthew 6:31-33)

I knew all of this, but I had somehow slipped into seeking my own way. I need reminders like this from time to time to keep my focus and motives pure and clear. I received this word, repented, and rested in His presence. Then a vision came. I was driving a commercial bus through the parking lot of some major tourist attraction. The way was very difficult. There were buses everywhere. Many had parked a long distance away, because they didn't know they could get closer. Some had parked a little closer, but had stopped short because they had reached an area that provided what they desired – what they were seeking. I was struggling to navigate the bus through the narrow passageways between the parked buses, trees, and curbs. I examined my motives. I asked myself where I was trying to go and why. I heard the cry of my heart, "I just want to get closer to Him! I just want to be in His presence!" Each time I focused on Him the driving was easy. But, when I focused on me the driving was difficult.

At first, I thought the bus was empty, and I wondered why I was driving such a large vehicle to get to my destination. I wondered why I was driving a vehicle that I was so unfamiliar with at the time. The Lord was teaching me an important lesson. I should be very familiar with the ways and means of getting to Him. I should be so accustomed to this journey that it would be easy. But, I keep trying to rely on myself, and the only way to get through is to rely on Him. As I realized this, I was suddenly aware that the bus was not empty. You and many others were on the bus with me. All those who are committed to seeking Him were on the way to His presence. When we make that desire to be with Him our first priority, the way becomes clear and smooth. I wanted a word for you, but He wanted you to find the way to Him. I wanted a word for me, but He wanted me to find the way to Him.

When I am fully in His presence, I have no questions to be answered, needs to be met, or things to be desired. When I am with Him in heavenly places, all I want is Him. I am completely satisfied with Him. I do not want or need anything but Him. When we can come to Him like this all the other things we need will be added unto us. We don't have to beg or plead our case. He knows! He loves! He blesses! He gives! May you and I seek first the kingdom of God continually and trust Him to provide what we need! May we have a heart hunger to be in His presence that is so strong that any desire for "presents" is lost from our awareness! May we just seek Him and find rest in Him! Amen!

———————————

DAY 19

HIS PRESENCE BRINGS PEACE

Today, the Lord made a much stronger call on my heart to pray for Israel and to pray for Korea. As I prayed, the Lord put it into my heart to pray the words given to Isaiah concerning Messiah found in Isaiah 11:2. I was instructed to pray this for Israel and Korea: *"The Spirit of the Lord shall rest upon Him, The Spirit of wisdom and understanding, The Spirit of counsel and might, The Spirit of knowledge and of the fear of the LORD."* (Isaiah 11:2) In my intercessory warfare over these two nations, I prayed for God to let the Spirit of the Lord rest now upon these two nations in all the manifestations revealed through Isaiah the prophet. There is great need today in both nations for wisdom, understanding, counsel, might, knowledge, and the fear of the Lord. Both nations are keys to the beginning of the great end-time harvest which is now at hand.

After praying this prayer, I was caught up into the third heaven and was bowing before the throne of Jesus. It was an awesome and majestic scene. The throne was so high and Jesus was so high and lifted up over the throne. I worshipped and gave thanksgiving and praise to Him. I was expecting Him to say something that would relate to the message for today, but He silently looked over His kingdom and His people. There was a great peace about Him and He had a look of satisfaction on His face. This was awesome considering some of the things going on in His church today.

Then the message of yesterday came back to my spirit. I knew that all I wanted was Him. I am seeking His face. I desire most His presence. What more could I desire that this? So, I just worshipped Him. As I gave honor, glory, majesty and praise to Him, a great sense of peace came over me. I was so content to be in His presence. I knew that this is the ultimate desire of the born again spirit – to just be with Him.

As I was allowed to continue in His presence, He stretched out His arms with His palms facing upward and lovingly said, "Come to me!" Others began to join me before the Lord. I was aware that you were there as well. After a time, He again reached out to others saying, "Come to me!" His voice was very loving and carried the powerful message of His desire to have His bride with him. More came and we worshipped together before the Lord. Then a third time He stretched forth His hands making a stronger plea, and saying, *"Come to Me, all you who labor and are heavy laden, and I will give you rest. Take My yoke upon you and learn from Me, for I am gentle and lowly in heart, and you will find rest for your souls. For My yoke is easy and My burden is light."* (Matthew 11:28-30) More came and worshipped the Lord.

Each time more came, the Lord's joy increased. I noticed that my joy increased as well. Then I became aware that in His presence – in the intimacy of our worship before Him – we truly begin to feel what He feels – to love what He loves – to care for what He desires. This is such an awesome thought. I know this is what it means to have the heart of Jesus. This is what Paul was talking about when he said, *"But we all, with unveiled face, beholding as in a mirror the glory of the Lord, are being transformed into the same image from glory to glory, just as by the Spirit of the Lord."* (2 Corinthians 3:18) As we are in Him and as He is in us, we truly begin to see His glory reflected in our own image.

May you go "from glory to glory just as by the Spirit of the Lord!" May you experience being in His presence today fully in union with Him worshipping in the beauty of Holiness! May the very image of the glory of Christ be reflected in you today so that all you meet may be drawn to His presence and enter into His worship! Amen!

DAY 20

SEEING AN OPEN HEAVEN

T his morning, the Lord gave me an awesome vision of an open heaven. As I looked into the opening a powerful release of His glory poured out toward earth. It looked like a giant Asian fan being thrown open. The fan looked like blazing fire with a radiant amber color. All of this was being poured out toward all who were willing to receive it. As I thought about telling you about this experience, the Lord said, "Many people do not understand what you are talking about when you speak of an open heaven, because they have not yet seen it or experienced it. Don't be surprised that they don't understand your words. Pray for their eyes to be opened to see all that the Father has for them and that their ears will be opened to hear what He is saying to them today."

Just as suddenly, I was enveloped in darkness as a large crowd of people fled back from the open heaven sweeping me away with them. The opening grew smaller and smaller and it felt like I was being pulled into the darkness of a cave instead of moving toward the light of the opening. I did not like being pulled back into the darkness with the fear of the unknown growing stronger and stronger in the people around me. Then I heard the voice of the Lord saying, "An open heaven causes some people to fear and they want to flee from it. They experience something like Adam and Eve who took their eyes off the Lord after eating the fruit of the tree of the knowledge of good and evil. They looked at themselves instead of the glory of God and realized that they were naked. When you look to yourself instead of to the glory of God, you will be tempted to hide as they did out of a fear of judgment. This fear is not the same as the righteous fear of God."

65

I was so pleased to break free from this darkness and get back into the light. As I immerged into the light, I saw a vision of numerous sets of strong strings sent forth from the open heaven toward earth. These strings looked like gigantic piano or guitar strings. As I watched, I saw that something was flowing down the strings, but I couldn't quite understand what it was. Then the Lord said, "I am releasing new music from heaven for those who love and desire to give praise to Father God. Much of what is called worship music today is more performance than praise. Many worship leaders have been deceived into seeking celebrity status and are writing and performing music out of their natural hearts. When the most frequent words in the songs are "I", "me", and "my", then you will know that it is more performance than praise. So, I am sending the music from heaven to those who desire to praise me rather than getting praise, glory, and honor for themselves."

I hesitated to send this message out. I said to the Lord, "You know there are some who will not receive this message well." After a long pause, the Lord reminded me that He admonishes those He loves. He assured me that this was a message of love and not of judgment. If we focus on ourselves, we tend to get offended. Jesus said again, *"And blessed is he who is not offended because of Me."* (Matthew 11:6, Luke 7:23) We are lovingly admonished to consider our worship and how we most often focus. We know that we must:

> *"Make a joyful shout to the Lord, all you lands! Serve the Lord with gladness; Come before His presence with singing. Know that the Lord, He is God; It is He who has made us, and not we ourselves; we are His people and the sheep of His pasture. Enter into His gates with thanksgiving, And into His courts with praise. Be thankful to Him, and bless His name. For the Lord is good; His mercy is everlasting, and His truth endures to all generations.* (Psalm 100)

May you not be offended by any admonishment that comes from the Lord! May you know His loving kindness so well that you welcome His discipline which leads to better discipleship! May your heart be filled with His praise! May you hear the new songs being released from heaven and experience a deeper level of worship than you have ever known! May all your worship and praise bless the Lord and give Him honor, praise, glory, and majesty! Amen!!!! If you are one who has never seen an open heaven, I pray that God will give you a glorious vision of it. May your eyes be opened as the eyes of Elisha's servant Gahazi to see clearly in the spirit realm.

> *"So he answered, "Do not fear, for those who are with us are more than those who are with them." And Elisha prayed, and said, "LORD, I pray, open his eyes that he may see." Then the LORD opened the eyes of the young man, and he saw. And behold, the mountain was full of horses and chariots of fire all around Elisha."* (2 Kings 6:16-17)

May you know with certainty that, *"You are of God, little children, and have overcome them, because He who is in you is greater than he who is in the world."* (1 John 4:4) May you see and receive from the storehouse of heaven everything that the Lord is pouring out for you today and always! Amen!

DAY 21

PRAY FOR THE HARVEST

Yesterday, as I prayed for our spiritual daughter in Korea, I saw a large number 8 hovering over her church. It looked like a blazing fire of radiant amber color hovering over the church as a proclamation of a new era. The number 8 is the prophetic number of new beginnings. It is the number 7 (the number of completeness of one era) plus 1 which is the first number of a new era. There were 8 people on Noah's ark with a destiny to establish a new beginning for the history of man. Abraham received 8 covenants of the Lord to establish a new nation of priests for the world. God commanded that circumcision be done on the eighth day symbolizing a life with a new beginning dedicated to the Lord.

This morning, I was again given the vision over South Korea and shown again the great spiritual warfare occurring in the body of the church located there. Then I saw the number 8 over the entire nation and heard a proclamation of a new era. The Lord said that this was the third era in the Korean church. The first era was the Era of Evangelism which built up the church to the level of critical mass and initiated the second great era. This second era was the Era of moving in the Holy Spirit with the accompanying gifts of the Spirit and prophecy. Now a new era is opening and it is the Era of End-time Harvest. This era is meeting with great resistance from the enemy because it signals the end of his reign on earth. The enemy's great desire is to delay this era and prolong his time of dominion.

The Lord has shown me the tactic of the enemy to accomplish his mission. He wants to distract the church from its destiny and purpose by getting people to look at themselves

and to seek their own will and purposes. This move will produce much distraction through jealousy, false accusations, and
growing rebellion by those under the influence of the Jezebel
spirit. Jesus warned the church about this time in His letter
to the church at Thyatira. All seven of the churches receiving
messages from the Lord in the Book of Revelation represent
the church age in which we currently live.

> *"Nevertheless I have a few things against you,*
> *because you allow that woman Jezebel, who*
> *calls herself a prophetess, to teach and seduce*
> *My servants to commit sexual immorality and*
> *eat things sacrificed to idols. And I gave her time*
> *to repent of her sexual immorality, and she did*
> *not repent."* (Revelation 2:20-21)

The Lord will not allow a church to tolerate the Jezebel spirit.
It must be cast out. This does not mean kicking people out, but
casting this spirit out of the church. If those manifesting this
spirit do not repent they too must leave the church. Remember
that sexual immorality in addition to actual sin is symbolic of the
idolatrous actions of worshiping the creation rather than the creator (see the book of Hosea). Then Jesus gives the key promise:

> *"Now I say to the rest of you in Thyatira, to*
> *you who do not hold to her teaching and have*
> *not learned Satan's so-called deep secrets (I*
> *will not impose any other burden on you):*
> *Only hold on to what you have until I come.*
> *To him who overcomes and does my will to*
> *the end, I will give authority over the nations"*
> (Revelation 2:24-26, NIV)

This is the prophetic word for South Korea and any other
nation willing to serve the Lord in this new era. It is to have

power over the nations (spiritually). The fires of the end-time harvest will burst forth from South Korea and spread like wildfire throughout the world at the end of the age. However, Korea and the other nations must hold fast to the true doctrine of Jesus and be led by the Holy Spirit while casting out the spirit of Jezebel.

As I continued this vision over the South Korean peninsula, very large spiritual hands were handing out food on trays. The food looked like French fries, and I marveled that the Lord would give fried foods to the people. I was quickly corrected and told that this was manna from heaven. The Lord said this was a fulfillment of the promise in Revelation 2:17, *"He who has an ear, let him hear what the Spirit says to the churches. To him who overcomes I will give some of the hidden manna to eat. And I will give him a white stone, and on the stone a new name written which no one knows except him who receives it,"*

As I watched, true believers were grasping large amounts of manna and placing it on their own plates. However the amount coming from heaven was not diminished. This spoke of the great abundance of provision that the Lord is offering to those who are willing to stand for Him in this time of spiritual warfare. We must understand that in the end those with Christ will overcome. Paul said,

> *"Finally, my brethren, be strong in the Lord and in the power of His might. Put on the whole armor of God, that you may be able to stand against the wiles of the devil. For we do not wrestle against flesh and blood, but against principalities, against powers, against the rulers of the darkness of this age, against spiritual hosts of wickedness in the heavenly places. Therefore take up the whole armor of God, that you may be able to withstand in the evil day, and having done all, to stand."* (Ephesians 6:10-13)

May all who have received the call to intercessory prayer for Korea be encouraged by these prophetic revelations from the Lord! May all who are praying for the Lord to release revival in their nations hear the call to intercede in prayer right now! May your commitment to pray for the end-time harvest be strengthened and increased! May you receive hidden manna as you hold fast to what the Lord has given you! Amen!

DAY 22

KEEP YOUR EYES ON JESUS!

After singing, giving thanks, praising, worshipping, and inter-
ceding for nations and individuals, I asked the Holy Spirit
to tell me what heaven is saying today. I prayed for this word from
heaven, because I desire to see what the Father is doing so I can
do that. I want to hear what the Father is saying so I can say that.

As I prayed, I went into an open vision. I saw a window in
heaven that I had never seen before. It was a very large window
shaped like a perfect circle. I noticed a frame inside the window
dividing it into 4 sections. At first I thought that the window had
panes (pains) in it, but I was reminded that the Lord makes rich and
adds no sorrow (pains) with it. As I examined the frame, I noticed
that the four openings were not the same size. Then I saw that the
frame in the middle of the window was in the shape of a cross.
When I saw it, a great outpouring of the Shekinah glory of God
poured forth as a purple-bluish cloud. Hebrews 12:2 came into my
mind, *"looking unto Jesus, the author and finisher of our faith, who
for the joy that was set before Him endured the cross, despising the
shame, and has sat down at the right hand of the throne of God."*

I heard the Lord saying, "You asked to see what I am doing
so you can do it! Keep your eyes fixed on Jesus! See what He
did because He only did what He saw me doing! More than
that, you can witness in the spirit what He is doing now and
do it." I was reminded of John 5:19, *"Then Jesus answered
and said to them, "Most assuredly, I say to you, the Son can
do nothing of Himself, but what He sees the Father do; for
whatever He does, the Son also does in like manner."*

"You asked to hear what I am saying so you can say it! Go
to the Word and read what Jesus said and say the same thing.

He only said what He heard me saying." John 12:49-50, *"For I have not spoken on My own authority; but the Father who sent Me gave Me a command, what I should say and what I should speak. And I know that His command is everlasting life. Therefore, whatever I speak, just as the Father has told Me, so I speak."* Then I heard the Lord say, "If you say what He said, you are saying what I am saying!"

"In addition, you can hear Him in the Spirit and say what He is saying! But, you have to stay in the Word. That is the only way you will recognize His voice. You must know His voice to follow Him!" John 10:3-5 (NIV), *"The watchman opens the gate for him, and the sheep listen to his voice. He calls his own sheep by name and leads them out. When he has brought out all his own, he goes on ahead of them, and his sheep follow him because they know his voice. But they will never follow a stranger; in fact, they will run away from him because they do not recognize a stranger's voice."*

Again, I looked at the window in heaven and I could see more clearly the need to stay focused on Jesus, the living Word of God, and to stay in the written Word of God. Philippians 3:13-14, *"Brethren, I do not count myself to have apprehended; but one thing I do, forgetting those things which are behind and reaching forward to those things which are ahead, I press toward the goal for the prize of the upward call of God in Christ Jesus."* If we want to live under an open heaven, we must keep our eyes on Jesus. The heavens have been torn open over Him. Mark 1:10-11 (AMP), *"And when He came up out of the water, at once he* [John] *saw the heavens torn open and the [Holy] Spirit like a dove coming down* [to enter into Him]. *And there came a voice out from within heaven, You are My beloved Son; in You I am well pleased."* Like John, look up and see that the heavens have been torn open over Jesus. Get close to Him and live under that open heaven. Amen!

DAY 23

A FLOOD OF LIVING WATER

This morning, I visited a part of the Lord's garden in heaven. It was such a beautiful place. It was similar to a meadow with plush green grass covering the ground like a carpet. The sky was a beautiful blue with puffy white clouds outlining the expanse and giving it definition. The temperature was perfect and the air was crystal clear. I was aware of a strong presence of the Lord and occasionally caught a glimpse of the Shekinah glory cloud moving through the meadow with me. I began a tour of the perimeter which was lined with a beautiful forest. All of the trees were crystal clear and perfectly arranged to give beauty and privacy to this special place of meeting with the Lord. Each part of the woods encircling the meadow was unique, beautiful, quiet, peaceful, and safe. My soul was at complete rest and peace while my spirit was so alive and energized as I delighted in the presence of the Lord.

As I continued on my journey around the forest lined meadow, I came to a place where there was an opening in the trees. I waited in this spot expecting a divine visitation. As I looked with expectancy through the trees, I was suddenly surprised by a mighty rushing flood of waters coming toward me with great speed and force. My first reaction was surprise and concern about being swept away. But these feelings were quickly dismissed as the waters rushed over me without any harm or pressure to wash me away. My first thought was of Isaiah 59:19b, *"When the enemy comes in – like a flood, the Spirit of the LORD will lift up a standard against him."* This heavenly flood was a rushing in of the Holy Spirit in power.

As the waters passed by, I was aware that I had been washed clean, renewed, and made ready to meet with the Lord. Wow! What an awesome feeling. I was reminded of what the Lord said to Moses in Numbers 8:5-7a, *"The Lord said to Moses: 'Take the Levites from among the other Israelites and make them ceremonially clean. To purify them, do this: Sprinkle the water of cleansing on them;'"* I received a lot more than a sprinkling. I felt like I had gone through the Lord's "Spirit, Soul, and Body Wash." As I turned to spend time with the Lord, He reminded me of His words in John 7:37-38, *"On the last day, that great day of the feast, Jesus stood and cried out, saying, "If anyone thirsts, let him come to Me and drink. He who believes in Me, as the Scripture has said, out of his heart will flow rivers of living water."* This river of living water had washed away every hurt, disappointment, injury, and offense. It had washed away everything that hindered my relationship with the Lord.

We all have this to look forward to when we dwell with Him forever, and He wants us to experience as much of it as possible while we are still here in the body, when we need it so much. Give thanks to our God and Father who gives so generously and abundantly (not just a sprinkling, but a flood)! Give thanks to our Lord Jesus who made it possible! Give thanks to the Holy Spirit who brings it to us and completes the work in us!

May you experience this joy of the Lord to be healed, cleansed, set free, and filled with the living water! May the flood waters wash over you and take away all pain, offense, disappointment, and loneliness! May He fill you with living water to empower you to spread the blessing to others who are in need! May you be filled and covered with the oil of joy! May you walk closely with the Lord today and enjoy that fellowship in a renewed and more glorious way than ever before! Amen!

FILLING THE STOREHOUSE

This morning I went before the Lord with such a strong hunger for His presence that I just kept crying out to see Him more clearly, to know Him more deeply, and to hear Him more clearly. I felt His presence so strongly and the room was charged like a field of static electricity. I felt like I was immersed in His presence and His life giving power was flowing through me.

As I lay face down in His presence soaking it up like a sponge, I went into an open vision. I saw a magnificent snow-capped mountain rising high into the sky gently touching the clouds above. It was beautiful and I was taking it all in when I noticed that smoke was rising from the top of the mountain. It looked like the Indian smoke signals from the old western movies. Then I heard the voice of the Lord telling me that He is sending out a signal to His people. It is a warning to stay alert and be prepared for His next move in the Spirit. I heard the Holy Spirit saying, "Prepare now, because a time of famine is coming. Fill up your storehouse with what you need most! Fill the storehouse of your heart with the Word of God! It is food for your souls and will fully equip you for the challenging times which are coming." A scripture came into my mind:

> *"And take the helmet of salvation, and the sword*
> *of the Spirit, which is the word of God; praying*
> *always with all prayer and supplication in the*
> *Spirit, being watchful to this end with all perse-*
> *verance and supplication for all the saints—and*
> *for me, that utterance may be given to me, that*

I may open my mouth boldly to make known the mystery of the gospel, for which I am an ambassador in chains; that in it I may speak boldly, as I ought to speak." (Ephesians 6:17-20)

A time is coming when more boldness will be needed as we share the mysteries of the gospel with a world becoming more and more hostile to those who follow Jesus Christ. A time is coming when we will need the Word of God in our hearts and minds and not just in a book on the shelf. Begin to fill the storehouse of your heart with the Word of God so that when the time of need comes, you will be prepared to skillfully use the "sword of the Spirit."

As I hear others speaking of the last days, I hear a call to store up food for the body. That is important. We do need food. However, we need faith more than food. We must be prepared to live by faith rather than by the abundance of physical things we store up. And, we know how to build up our faith. "So then faith *comes* by hearing, and hearing by the word of God." (Romans 10:17) Good soldiers train and prepare before the battle begins. Once the battle begins, it is too late to train up and be ready. Wise spiritual warriors are training up NOW! Wise disciples are getting prepared NOW!

As I continued to watch the smoke rising from the mountaintop, I was reminded of what Jesus said in Matthew 24:42, *"Watch therefore, for you do not know what hour your Lord is coming."* I remember the words of Peter as he quoted Joel in Acts chapter two:

"In the last days, God says, I will pour out my Spirit on all people. Your sons and daughters will prophesy, your young men will see visions, your old men will dream dreams. Even on my servants, both men and women, I will pour out my Spirit in those days, and they will prophesy. I

will show wonders in the heaven above and signs on the earth below, blood and fire and billows of smoke." (Acts 2:17-19, NIV)

There will be wonders in the heaven above and signs on the earth below. One of the signs will be billows of smoke. That was what I saw on the mountains in the vision this morning. The signal has been given and it is time to make preparataions. *"Who then is a faithful and wise servant, whom his master made ruler over his household, to give them food in due season? Blessed is that servant whom his master, when he comes, will find so doing. Assuredly, I say to you that he will make him ruler over all his goods."* (Matthew 24:45-47, NIV)

May the Lord always find you prepared and ready for His next move in the Spirit! May the Lord find you doing what He has given you to do! May the Lord be so pleased with your service that He entrusts you with more! May you be preparing now by filling the storehouse of your heart with the Word of God. Amen!!!

DAY 25

RENEWING OLD BARNS

This morning the Lord gave me a vision of a beautiful rural scene with tree lined, fertile fields and an old barn in the center of the picture. As I looked at the barn, it began to change and become new. Over a short period of time, it was strengthened, renewed, repainted, and built up into a strong and impressive structure. Now, let me explain something. This is very special to me, because I really enjoy looking at old barns. I have a collection of pictures of old barns on my computer and some worship videos which use old barns as a background.

When I look at an old barn, I see so much more than the building. I see the hopes and dreams of people in the near and distant past. I see them laboring hard to build up an abundance of supply to feed both animals and human beings. The size and beauty of the dreams is reflected in the type and size of the barn. You can see so much of what the past brought to a previous generation by the age, condition, and magnitude of the barn. I know that barns are representations of our hopes and dreams for our families and our ministries. So, this vision had special meaning for me, and I hope the Holy Spirit can communicate that to you.

As I watched the transition of the barn, the Holy Spirit reminded me of Matthew 13:52, "*Then He said to them, "Therefore every scribe instructed concerning the kingdom of heaven is like a householder who brings out of his treasure things new and old*." The Lord said that many good things are in our old structures and we need to hold on to them. In our attempts to rid ourselves of the spirit of religion we must not throw out the baby with the bath water. We need to discern between what is good and what is not helpful, and learn to let go of (throw out) what is no longer useful. At the same time, we need to add the new things which the Lord is giving us through the ministry of the Holy Spirit. If we are wise in the kingdom of heaven, we will learn to blend the old and the new into the very fabric of our lives and our ministries. Then the Lord asked me to impart again the Word given through Isaiah:

> *"There shall come forth a Rod from the stem of Jesse, and a Branch shall grow out of his roots. The Spirit of the LORD shall rest upon Him, The Spirit of wisdom and understanding, The Spirit of counsel and might, The Spirit of knowledge and of the fear of the LORD."* (Isaiah 11:1-2)

As the Spirit of the Lord rested on Yeshua ha Messiah during His ministry on earth, He released this same Spirit to us in order to empower, guide, and teach us during these last days. As I reflected on this instruction, I remembered a documentary on the strategies of movie making. Today, many movie makers insert sequences into their productions which accelerate the speed in the scene to make it look like things are coming at you very quickly. This draws the attention of viewers and brings them into sharp focus in preparation for a key scene.

In the same way, the Lord is now accelerating time, drawing our attention to the end of days. He is drawing our focus back on what is needed to prepare us for this time. This acceleration draws us back to some key scenes like the release of the Spirit of the Lord on the ministry of Jesus. It draws us into the scene where we can receive impartation of this same Spirit of the Lord with the accompanying wisdom, understanding, counsel, might, knowledge, and fear of the Lord.

I pray that you will be open today to receive a greater impartation of the Spirit of the Lord! I pray that you will be strengthened, built up, and renewed for your role in the unfolding revelation of the kingdom of God! I pray that the acceleration of these days will draw your focus away from trivial pursuits and back onto the key movements of the kingdom of God. I pray that you will receive all of the empowerment you need for the call on your life and to reach your destiny in God's service! Amen!

———————————

DAY 26

DRESSING THE BRIDE

I got a late start this morning. After the awesome outpouring we had last night in our soaking service, I was unable to sleep until well after midnight. God's presence was so strong that it was like moving into a huge field of powerful static electricity. We felt the fire of His glory and received visions, revelations, and a great outpouring of His love along with impartation of gifts and increases in the power of existing gifts. Oil from heaven physically manifested in the palms of our hands. Wow! What an awesome God we serve!

This morning, as I entered His presence, I prayed for a release of greater truth through the Holy Spirit. I asked the Lord to reveal through the Holy Spirit what heaven is saying today – what is important in the kingdom of God and not just the world. After a time, I heard the Lord saying, "Wednesday is wedding day. It is an appointed time to rehearse for the Wedding Feast of the Lamb. It is a time for the bride to be prepared with fresh oil of anointing to be cleansed and made ready for her Groom. It is a time to put on the pure white garment – the righteousness of Jesus the Christ – and to wear the garment of praise He has so generously provided." Isaiah 61:3 (NIV), "*and provide for those who grieve in Zion—to bestow on them a crown of beauty instead of ashes, the oil of gladness instead of mourning, and a garment of praise instead of a spirit of despair. They will be called oaks of righteousness, a planting of the LORD for the display of his splendor.*"

The Lord continued, "It is time to be bejeweled with all the adornments of the Lord." I saw twenty four jewels being attached to the wedding garment. First there were the twelve jewels representing the twelve tribes of Israel like the ones worn on the priest's vestments. Then twelve more were added for the elders of the church of Jesus Christ so that the total would represent the twenty four elders before the throne of God. Isaiah 61:10 (NIV), *"I delight greatly in the LORD; my soul rejoices in my God. For he has clothed me with garments of salvation and arrayed me in a robe of righteousness, as a bridegroom adorns his head like a priest, and as a bride adorns herself with her jewels."*

Most believers desire to be the bride of Christ, but many are not willing to pay the price required to be prepared for the Bridegroom. Esther spent an entire year in preparation for one night with the King. Esther 2:12, *"Each young woman's turn came to go in to King Ahasuerus after she had completed twelve months' preparation, according to the regulations for the women, for thus were the days of their preparation apportioned: six months with oil of myrrh, and six months with perfumes and preparations for beautifying women."* In a day of fast food, fast cars, fast technology, and fast service, who is willing to spend the time to be prepared? Who will give a day much less a year to prepare for the day of the Lord?

The Lord provides everything: the wedding garment, the perfumed oils, the wedding ceremony, the celebration feast, and an eternal home with His Father in heaven. What are you willing to do? What are you willing to provide? All He asks is that we present ourselves as living sacrifices. He doesn't require great abilities – just our willing availability. May you spend this day as a time of true preparation for the return of the Bridegroom and the great Wedding Feast of the Lamb! May you put on the garments of righteousness after soaking in the perfumed oils of heaven! May you put on the jewels He provides, and ready yourself for Him! May you be filled with love, excitement, and joy at the prospect of seeing Jesus very soon! Amen!

DAY 27

SELF - REPLENISHING PROVISION

This morning, the Lord gave me a series of visions and heavenly experiences. First, I had a vision of a large, well worn, overstuffed chair with several fluffy pillows made from a matching fabric. The color of the chair and the pillows was a powder blue. On the armrest of the chair was an open Bible which had been carefully placed as though someone reading it had been called away. On the chair cushion was a heavy antique silver necklace with a matching ornamental cross. The Lord said, "To come into my presence you have to leave everything behind – even your most precious things."

Those who know me are aware that the Bible and the cross are my two most precious items. Even these must be left behind when we go to the third heaven to be with the Lord. That is still a difficult concept for me. I just don't want to let go of these. Then I realized that I want to be with the Lord more than I want even these most precious things. Philippians 3:13-14 (NIV), "*Brothers, I do not consider myself yet to have taken hold of it. But one thing I do: Forgetting what is behind and straining toward what is ahead, I press on toward the goal to win the prize for which God has called me heavenward in Christ Jesus.*"

As I more fully understood this concept of leaving everything behind, I was lifted up into heaven into a room in our Father's house. I was in one of the mansions Jesus promised to prepare for us (John 14:2-3). In this room, I saw some who had been lifted up to heaven for the first time. The joy and excitement being displayed through these people was inspirational. Their faces were covered with expressions of joy and I saw wide smiles on every face. Some were bringing their hands over their mouths in gestures expressing overwhelming surprise and joy that they had finally broken free of every hindrance and were now in heavenly places with the Lord. Two came near me and spoke with joyous voices filled with extreme excitement saying, "I am finally here in my heavenly home!" Wow! It was just awesome to watch the excitement and joy they were experiencing on this first visit. They were literally dancing with joy. Psalm 5:11, *"But let all those rejoice who put their trust in You; Let them ever shout for joy, because You defend them; Let those also who love Your name be joyful in You."*

As I celebrated their joy with them, we were moved into a large banquet hall. Huge tables were filled with delicious food piled high on large silver trays. The hot dishes were steaming hot to perfection, and the cold dishes were at the perfect temperature. As we took food from the trays, they were immediately replenished from within. I heard the Lord declare, "Self-replenishing provision is given to you. You never need to fear lack again!" Even as we experienced the amazement of this wonderful place, ministering spirits were bringing out more trays. Every type of food anyone could desire was being brought out and presented to us. As new people arrived, their favorite foods were delivered. I kept holding on to that word from the Lord: "self-replenishing provision." Then I was led to Isaiah 25:6 (NIV), *"On this mountain the Lord Almighty will prepare a feast of rich food for all peoples, a banquet of aged wine—the best of meats and the finest of wines."*

More messages from the Word were given to me. Psalm 35:27, *"Let them shout for joy and be glad, who favor my righteous cause; and let them say continually, 'Let the Lord be magnified, Who has pleasure in the prosperity of His servant.'"* God is so good, and desires most that His obedient children prosper, and be in health. Then I was given 3 John 1:2, *"Beloved,*

I pray that you may prosper in all things and be in health, just as your soul prospers." The Lord has so much good planned and prepared for you. So, leave everything behind and press in to be in His presence. Seek His face and He will be found!

May the Lord bless you with the joy of heavenly visitation! May you see and taste the banquet prepared by the Lord, and then know that He is good! His plan is to prosper you while He gives you hope and a future. May you trust in the Lord and receive the desires of your heart! Amen!

DAY 28

A TRUMPET ABOUT TO SOUND

All I can say this morning is, "Wow!" As I prayed for the Holy Spirit to teach me what heaven is saying today, a great desire to be in the Throne Room of heaven came into my heart and I cried out for it. I was immediately transported into the heavenly realm and had an amazingly brief trip through the Throne Room as I was ushered out to what I can only describe as a backyard barbeque. I quickly let go of my sense of missing the Throne Room experience I had requested, and got involved in the activities in the back yard of God's glorious mansion.

Excited and joyous people were assembling for this wonderful family outing. Smoke was rising from the cooking fires, and the smells of delicious foods being roasted over open fires flooded my senses. We were all waiting with great expectancy for the arrival of the guest of honor. People were sharing stories about all the marvelous things He has done, is doing, and will do in the future. The expectancy and excitement increased with every story shared about our wonderful Lord and Savior, Yeshua. I remember the words of Revelation 19:10b, "*I am your fellow servant, and of your brethren who have the testimony of Jesus. Worship God! For the testimony of Jesus is the spirit of prophecy.*"

There we were, brothers and sisters, receiving and sharing the testimonies of Jesus. And, these testimonies were releasing prophetic words. I heard in the spirit, "What Jesus has said in the past, he is saying now, and will say in the future. The truth never changes. What Jesus has done in the past, he is doing now, and will do in the future. His mercies never change." I realized that every shared story was building faith in the rest of us. We were saying in our hearts, "If He did that for them, He will do that for me! If He said that to them, He will say that to me!" Every prophetic word increased the sense of expectancy as we waited for His arrival. Revelation 1:8, *"I am the Alpha and the Omega, the Beginning and the End," says the Lord, "who is and who was and who is to come, the Almighty."* It was really an awesome experience in heaven. More than ever before, I heard my heart crying out the words of John in Revelation 22:20, *"He who testifies to these things says, "Surely I am coming quickly." Amen. Even so, come, Lord Jesus!"*

As I celebrated this experience and waited in joy for His arrival, the Holy Spirit guided me into this truth, "This is a foreshadowing of the Feast of Trumpets celebration in heaven (Rosh Hashanah)." The time is approaching to celebrate this feast (Hebrew: the word translated "feast" is actually "appointed time") of the Lord. It is an appointed time for the return of our Lord Jesus in power and great glory when we hear that last great trumpet (the *tekiah*). It is also a call to repentance as the shofar sounds the *teruah*; nine staccato blasts – the sound of brokenness. It ushers in a time of repentance in preparation for Yom Kippur; the day of Atonement. On the two days of this appointed time to meet with the Lord, it is traditional to eat apples dipped in honey, all kinds of sweet fruits, pome-granates, and *challah* bread (round loaves symbolizing crowns – pointing to the Lord's kingship).

When we meet the Lord at these appointed times, He gives great blessings to His faithful people. I understood that this visit was a direct invitation for us to join the celebration this year. We are encouraged to share our testimonies of Jesus. We are expected to release prophecy through the sharing of these testimonies. And with expectancy wait upon the Lord's return.

Some see this as a challenging time of reflecting on our mistakes and working out our salvation. But the experience in heaven painted a much different picture for those who are already redeemed of the Lord; those whose sins have already been atoned for by the death of Jesus. For the redeemed, it is a time of great joy, celebration, expectancy, and encouragement. May we spend these days lifting up our brothers and sisters, encouraging them, and giving words of comfort and assurance to those in need! Amen?

DAY 29

PRE-OPENING SHOPPING

After spending a couple of hours in the Word and moving into a time of praise and worship, I went into an open vision. In front of me was an overstuffed Queen Anne chair sitting beside a small table with a lamp which was giving a warm glow to the whole scene. There was an open Bible on the chair and it was obvious that someone had risen early to spend time studying the Word. Behind the chair a portal had opened in the wall revealing darkness on the outside of the house, because it was very early in the morning.

Suddenly, I was pulled through the portal and found myself standing in what appeared to be a grocery store. There were many very long rows of shelving filled with a wide variety of different types of supplies. The lights were not on in the store, but people were shopping freely in what appeared to be a pre-opening opportunity for special customers. Then I heard the Lord say, "This is one of the storerooms in heaven." This insight gave a whole new light on what was happening here in semi-darkness. I saw someone pick up a box of laundry detergent, and the Spirit showed me the label which said, "Savior Suds – the Redeemer's Soap." As I watched, this person was completely cleansed of all her past and set free to love and serve the Lord. Hallelujah! Then I saw another person picking up healing ointments, and immediately healing and restoration came over her. Next, I saw a man putting women's clothing in a garment bag. I wondered who the clothing was for, and then I saw him on a train looking at the dresses again. As I watched the Lord said that He was going on a mission trip and taking heavenly garments to those who would receive his ministry.

These were only a few of the many items in the store, and I was filled with expectancy about how many other wonderful things would be given into the lives of those in need.

The Lord explained to me the meaning of the pre-opening shopping. Those who serve the Lord have access to His storehouse night and day, every day. Those who walk by faith, can reach out at any time and take what they need for ministry. I wondered why we don't see more people going to this storehouse and getting what they need. The Lord said it was because they don't really believe they can. Too many of those who say they are believers are walking by sight and not by faith. This is backwards thinking in the logic of the kingdom of God. *"For we walk by faith, not by sight."* (2 Corinthians 5:7) I began to look around for a box or bottle of faith. I was sure it must be there somewhere, because, *"For it is by grace you have been saved, through faith—and this not from yourselves, it is the gift of God—not by works, so that no one can boast."* (Ephesians 2:8-9, NIV)

May you find the open portal giving you entrance into the storehouse of God! May you receive bountifully all that He has prepared and purposed for you! May you find the desires of your heart and then be blessed beyond what you have asked and imagined! May you walk by faith and not by sight, knowing that those things you have received in the spirit will soon manifest in the natural! Amen!

> *"'Bring all the tithes into the storehouse, that there may be food in My house, and try Me now in this,' says the Lord of hosts, 'If I will not open for you the windows of heaven and pour out for you such blessing that there will not be room enough to receive it. And I will rebuke the devourer for your sakes, so that he will not destroy the fruit of your ground, nor shall the vine fail to bear*

fruit for you in the field,' says the LORD of hosts;"
(Malachi 3:10-11)

DAY 30

READY OR NOT

This morning, as I gazed up into an open heaven, I saw what first appeared to be a giant, silver colored shower head being thrust through the opening. As I watched, I noticed that there was no water coming from it. As I pondered that for a few moments, a revelation was given from the Lord. It wasn't a shower head. It was a gigantic silver trumpet being readied to sound over the earth. This scene was replaced by a very large figure of someone dressed in priestly robes raising a shofar and preparing to sound the call to an assembly.

> *"For the Lord Himself will descend from heaven with a shout, with the voice of an archangel, and with the trumpet of God. And the dead in Christ will rise first. Then we who are alive and remain shall be caught up together with them in the clouds to meet the Lord in the air. And thus we shall always be with the Lord. Therefore comfort one another with these words."*
> (1 Thessalonians 4:16-18)

The Spirit helped me understand that there were two messages just as there had been two trumpets. The first message is a call to be prepared for the Lord's Feast of Trumpets coming soon. I heard questions being asked of us. "Are you ready? Have you made your preparations?" The people of God have always been asked to consecrate themselves before their appointments to meet with the Lord. There needs to be a period of repentance, cleansing, and dressing in appropriate attire. Are you ready for your appointment this year?

The second message revealed by the Holy Spirit is that this is a time of preparation for the great end-time trumpet call. I heard the Lord saying, "Are you ready for my return? Have you prepared yourself? Have you invited others to come?" I became aware of how we have heard this message so many times that we run the risk of not being on the cutting edge of the final movement. We may be lulled to sleep by the enemy who sows doubt and attempts to veil our eyes from what God is preparing to do. Are you ready if Jesus returns for His church on this Feast of Trumpets? Luke 12:40, *"Therefore you also be ready, for the Son of Man is coming at an hour you do not expect."*

Then I saw a great assembly of people gathering for the arrival of the Lord. The atmosphere was buzzing with excitement and expectancy. The voices of the people sounded something like instruments being tuned before the performance of a great symphony. This was both a grand fellowship of true believers and a time of making the instruments ready to sound His praises. I began to smell the fragrance of food being prepared and made ready for a great banquet in heaven.

As I watched with expectancy, a commotion arose. It seemed so out of place here in this heavenly assembly. The commotion began to move in my direction. Then I saw the source of the disturbance. Two very large ushers were each holding the arm of a man who was reluctantly being escorted out. He was not dressed in the robe of righteousness or the garment of praise so graciously provided by our Lord, Jesus.

> *"But when the king came in to see the guests, he saw a man there who did not have on a wedding garment. So he said to him, 'Friend, how did you come in here without a wedding garment?' And he was speechless. Then the king said to the*

servants, 'Bind him hand and foot, take him away,
and cast him into outer darkness; there will be
weeping and gnashing of teeth.' 'For many are
called, but few are chosen.'" (Matthew 22:11-14)

As I watched this man being escorted out where he was
shackled to an exterior wall, my eyes fell on another man
outside the door in a dark place. He was on his knees crying
because he had no garments except for a loin cloth. His upper
body and legs were bare and he was not allowed entrance. He
didn't seem to have any idea where to get garments. He was
kneeling, but not praying. He was crying, but not unto the
Lord. I thought, "The poor man. Even in these final moments,
he has no idea what to do in order to get prepared." Matthew
8:12, *"But the sons of the kingdom will be cast out into outer*
darkness. There will be weeping and gnashing of teeth."

Then I realized that each of the two men who were not
allowed into the assembly represented countless millions of
others. I felt convicted by the question, "What have you been
doing to help others like these to prepare for the feast?" Are
you ready for the Lord's return? God is so gracious to give us
more time. I pray that we will use it wisely and productively
for His kingdom on earth! Amen!

DAY 31

DOUBLE PORTION BLESSINGS

This morning, we needed to rise early to make a trip with friends to Moravian Falls. In order to arrive in time for the prayer meeting, we needed to leave home by 5:15 a.m. We planned to spend our time with the Lord on Prayer Mountain. So, I apologized to the Lord for being in a rush, and asked if there was a Word from heaven this morning. The Lord said the message was in the dream.

As I awakened I was having a very interesting dream. The scene shifted from place to place as I met with various people to pray for God's provision. Each time of prayer was in secluded areas of a parking lot. As I prayed with each person, their car doubled in size. After telling me that the message was in the dream, the Holy Spirit revealed that this was symbolic of double portion blessings coming for our ministries. The cars represented taking the ministry on the road and each was being miraculously increased by the Lord.

However, a strange thing was happening to the cars in the dream. Cars which had been left in the dark, secluded, and hidden areas of the parking lots were being stolen. We were told that we needed to move the cars to the front of the parking lot where the lights were bright and others could see them. The Holy Spirit guided me to understand that when we receive double portion blessings for ministry, we are to be up front with it. It is a testimony to others to accompany our ministry. Like David who promised to praise the Lord in front of the assembly each time the Lord provided for him, we too must be sure to use every blessing as a testimony to the Lord. I was given the following scriptures to guide our praise:

*"I will praise You, O LORD, with my whole heart;
I will tell of all Your marvelous works. I will be
glad and rejoice in You; I will sing praise to Your
name, O Most High."* (Psalm 9:1-2)

*"I will give You thanks in the great assembly; I will
praise You among many people."* (Psalm 35:18)

*"I will praise You, O Lord, among the peoples;
I will sing to You among the nations. For Your
mercy reaches unto the heavens, and Your truth
unto the clouds."* (Psalm 57:9-10)

Turn every blessing into praise! Rejoice in the Lord before the people, and make His name great among the nations! The Lord is so good, and others need to be encouraged by the testimonies of His people! Praise the Lord before everyone today and always! Amen! Remember James 1:17-18, *"Every good and perfect gift is from above, coming down from the Father of the heavenly lights, who does not change like shifting shadows. He chose to give us birth through the word of truth, that we might be a kind of firstfruits of all he created."*

DAY 32

EXTRAVAGANT REFRESHING

Today is a glorious day in heaven, and I suppose that every day is glorious there. However, today was special to me and I believe for you. I was blessed by the beauty of a star filled sky. The stars were passing overhead at a very high speed, and I was aware that an angelic host was passing before my eyes. The majesty and power of this time was inspirational and uplifting beyond description. The Lord then took me thought a series of experiences which were lessons for you and me.

Then the scene shifted into something I knew was for you; at least some of you. Someone walked toward me carrying a medium sized shopping bag. It was a very nice paper bag with two plastic loops for handles to carry it. I saw in crystal clear letters the words *"Arizona Tea"* on the front of the bag being carried in this person's left hand. In the person's right hand was an open bottle of Arizona Tea which was obviously being enjoyed by this person. The reason I feel sure that this was for you is that I don't drink Arizona Tea. I'm not really sure what it tastes like, but the person I saw was truly enjoying this experience.

As I watched this scene, I heard the Lord say, "I am releasing extravagant refreshing to my beloved people! I am not limiting your refreshing to just enough for you to hold out a little longer and stay in the battle a few more minutes. I will not only refresh and restore, but will elevate you to a higher level of blessing than you have ever known! I am lavishing refreshment, restoration, and exaltation on those who are open to receive it!"

> *"Jesus answered and said to her, "Whoever drinks of this water will thirst again, but who-ever drinks of the water that I shall give him will never thirst. But the water that I shall give him will become in him a fountain of water springing up into everlasting life." The woman said to Him, "Sir, give me this water, that I may not thirst, nor come here to draw."* (John 4:13-15)

At this point, I pressed in to receive it myself. Even though I knew this was for you, I wanted it for me as well. I am so hungry and so thirsty for the Lord. I began my worship this morning crying out to see His face. I cried out to be able to just soak in His presence. I cried out to just spend time with him in total devotion, worship, and love. So, when I heard this message, I was so happy for you, and I cried out to receive it for me as well. Matthew 5:6, *"Blessed are those who hunger and thirst for righteousness, for they shall be filled."* Reflect on the two passages below and assimilate their full meaning into your spirit and soul.

> *"And they did not thirst when He led them through the deserts; He caused the waters to flow from the rock for them; He also split the rock, and the waters gushed out."* (Isaiah 48:21)

> *"They all ate the same spiritual food and drank the same spiritual drink; for they drank from the spiritual rock that accompanied them, and that rock was Christ."* (1 Corinthians 10:3-4)

I pray that today you will be in touch with your extreme thirst for His presence, and that you will be called into His presence to receive this lavish gift of refreshing from your beloved Bridegroom! May your thirst be both satisfied and intensified, and may your level of refreshment rise to meet the level of your thirst! So, don't hold back! Press in for more and more! Amen?

———————————

DAY 33

FROM GOD'S PERSPECTIVE

This morning a vision came so fast that I almost missed it. My mind started to wander, but I stopped myself and asked the Holy Spirit if that was the message from heaven for today. The answer was, "Yes!" So, I asked to go back to the vision and learn the lessons. I was immediately taken back to that place. I was on a steep, straight, and long road leading up a very high mountain. Trees lined both sides of the road and all the leaves were in beautiful shades of green as in the early spring time. It seemed like a beautiful place for a vacation or day trip with the family to enjoy the outdoors and celebrate God's handiwork in creating such a beautiful place.

But, I had to stop because there was a checkpoint with a guardhouse in the middle of the road and barriers across the traffic lane. Some people were allowed to proceed and others were turned back. Obviously this was not an average mountain. There was something special about this place and only certain people were allowed to continue on the upward road. The Holy Spirit reminded me of Psalm Twenty Four.

> *"Who may ascend into the hill of the* Lord*? Or who may stand in His holy place? He who has clean hands and a pure heart, who has not lifted up his soul to an idol, nor sworn deceitfully. He shall receive blessing from the* Lord*, and righteousness from the God of his salvation. This is Jacob, the generation of those who seek Him, who seek Your face." Selah* (Psalm 24:3-6)

I learned that this was the mountain of the Lord, and only those cleansed by the blood of Jesus could continue up the road. Only people who were in the process of transforming their souls through the renewal of their minds were allowed to continue upward to His presence. The Holy Spirit reminded me of what Jesus said as recorded in John 4:23-24, *"But the hour is coming, and now is, when the true worshipers will worship the Father in spirit and truth; for the Father is seeking such to worship Him. God is Spirit, and those who worship Him must worship in spirit and truth."*

My only credentials were those given by Jesus, and I knew that I had a heart hunger to worship the Father in spirit and truth. In my heart, I have such a longing to be *"Jacob, the generation of those who seek Him, who seek Your face."* That was all that was needed. Passage was permitted, and I continued upward on the road, but the rate of speed dramatically increased. I was not in control of the vehicle I was in. This was a Holy Spirit controlled and Holy Spirit guided tour. I was extremely content with that truth. I earnestly desire for Him to be in control of my life. When I realized this, I felt like I was on top of the mountain looking around at the other mountain peaks. They were not covered with life and abundance like this mountain, but they were still magnificent in beauty because they were the creation of my Father God. Then I realized that I was not on top of the mountain. I was above it and looking down on it, and I was still ascending. Then from heaven I was looking down on all the beauty of God's creation. The mountain of the Lord was higher, covered with green trees, grass, and every form of vegetation. It was beautiful and awe inspiring. Then the Holy Spirit challenged me to meditate on this and find truth for today.

As I meditated, it came to me that from an earthly perspective the mountain had appeared huge and I was tiny by comparison. But from a heavenly perspective the mountain was small. What seems huge and immovable from our perspective in the flesh is but a small mound of easily moved dust from God's perspective. Suddenly a verse came to mind, *"For nothing is impossible with God."* (Luke 1:37, NIV) That verse made perfect sense. What we see as huge and foreboding is less than nothing to God. If we can rise above it all and see it from God's perspective, we can walk by faith and not by sight. We can live by faith and not by feelings, when we know that God can do anything and He has our best interests in His heart. This was an awesome revelation. I had known these things in my mind before, and now I knew them in my heart. Thank you, Father, God!

May you see things from God's perspective and put all your concerns at the feet of Jesus! May you have full assurance that God knows you, loves you, and has your best interests at heart! May you have full assurance that He not only can, but that He will provide what your need! May you truly walk by faith and not by sight or feelings! Amen!

DAY 34

PREPARING FOR HIS RETURN

T his experience occurred on the first day of the Feast of Trumpets. This is a new moon celebration in which we honor the Lord for all He has done for us through the salvation won by our savior Yeshua ha Messiah. We began our celebration last night at sundown by sounding the shofar and ram's horn over and over as we prepared our hearts for His return. The atmosphere was heavy with His weighty presence. As we lay on the floor before Him, it was as if a heavy weight had been placed over us from His presence. The Feast of Trumpets is an awesome time with the Lord, and it continues through sundown tomorrow. I pray that you will experience this weighty presence as well.

This morning in my worship time, I had trouble maintaining my focus. I attributed it to the enemy attempting to distract me from being fully focused on the presence of my Lord. So, I prayed the James 4:7 prayer several times and began to pray in the Spirit. Almost immediately, I had a vision of an expansive field of wheat nearing the time of harvest. The heads were full and beginning to change from green to golden brown. Thoughts of the great harvest at the end of the age immediately came to mind. I reflected on the vast number of Jewish people accepting Yeshua; the dividing wall coming down; and the joining of Jewish and Gentile believers into the one new man church. The thoughts were awesome and I was holding to them to share with you. Then suddenly, I was lifted out of that place and taken to the Throne Room of Heaven.

I saw Yeshua ha Messiah standing in heaven fully dressed in His majestic garments of white linen and gold sashes. He said, "Celebrate this appointed time as a rehearsal for my return!" I wondered how we could do that. He said, "Practice being ready and listening for the last great trumpet! Sound the trumpets as a reminder of the times and get used to the sound. Use this time to make your spirit ready and to move forward in transforming your soul through the renewal of your mind. The time is short. Sharpen your focus and be busily involved in my Father's business!" After saying this, the Lord started to move out for His final battle. As He came toward me, he looked directly at me and said, "Behold, I am coming soon!" I was immediately reminded that this is the third time He has told me that He is returning soon. Revelation 22:20, *"He who testifies to these things says, "Surely I am coming quickly." Amen. Even so, come, Lord Jesus!"*

This is not a season for doing business as usual. This is a season of acceleration in the kingdom of God. Now, is the time of preparation and the Lord reminds us that the time is short. Because we have heard this before, we may have a tendency to take it less seriously. However, remember that the Lord repeats things for emphasis. The more we hear it the more we should focus on the tasks to make ready for it. Genesis 41:32, *"And the dream was repeated to Pharaoh twice because the thing is established by God, and God will shortly bring it to pass."* In the same way, as Jesus repeats this truth about His return, we should understand that He is saying that it is established by God and He will shortly bring it to pass.

May you have a joyous celebrate with the Lord as you rehearse His great plan for us in the return of our Lord, Jesus Christ! May you find it pleasing to make preparations and stand watch for His return! May He find you ready and waiting when He comes! Even so, come quickly Lord Jesus! Amen!

DAY 35

HE IS COMING SOON

This morning, the Lord gave me a series of visions that came at such blinding speed that I cried out, "What was that? What just happened?" I knew that these visions had significant meaning, but they were just too fast. So, I asked the Holy Spirit to show me again and tell me what they meant. I was immediately taken back to the first vision and then slowly moved through each while the Holy Spirit guided my understanding.

The first vision was of a very high and rugged mountain peak. The scene was stark with no signs of life. Below me and all around the mountain peak were gathering clouds of deep darkness. It was as if some type of evil force was brooding over the face of the earth. The clouds were threatening and violent in their movement. The Holy Spirit said, "Perilous times will come as the end time harvest is ushered in, and many people will cower in fear at the threatened violence of that hour." I remembered the words of 2 Timothy 3:1-9, *"But know this, that in the last days perilous times will come: For men will be lovers of themselves, lovers of money, boasters, proud, blasphemers, disobedient to parents, unthankful, unholy, unloving, unforgiving, slanderers, without self-control, brutal, despisers of good, traitors, headstrong, haughty, lovers of pleasure rather than lovers of God, having a form of godliness but denying its power. And from such people turn away! For of this sort are those who creep into households and make captives of gullible women loaded down with sins, led away by various lusts, always learning and never able to come to the knowledge of the truth. Now as Jannes and Jambres resisted Moses, so do these also resist the truth: men of corrupt minds, disapproved concerning the faith; but they will progress no further, for their folly will be manifest to all, as theirs also was."* Through Paul, God has forewarned us of these times. Why should we be surprised by them?

While this was still sinking into my mind, the Holy Spirit carried me with him at blinding speed to a small boat being tossed about by huge waves in a troubled sea. From the natural this situation seemed hopeless. As if this was not a strong enough threat, the enemy threw a huge spear at the helpless people on the deck of the boat. The reason for the fast movement of the Holy Spirit had been for Him to arrive just in time to pull the people out of the path of the spear just as it passed harmlessly by them. In my mind I remembered the words of Isaiah 59:19b, *"When the enemy comes in, like a flood the Spirit of the LORD will lift up a standard against him."*

The Holy Spirit said, "This boat is a picture of the church. If the people of God look at the dark clouds, the storm, and the raging waves, they will be overcome by fear. But, what is impossible for man is possible for God. I am your shield during these perilous times at the end of the age. You too are called to be shields for the others. But, to do so, you must put on the whole armor of God every day."

> *"Stand therefore, having girded your waist with truth, having put on the breastplate of righteousness, and having shod your feet with the preparation of the gospel of peace; above all, taking the shield of faith with which you will be able to quench all the fiery darts of the wicked one. And take the helmet of salvation, and the sword of the Spirit, which is the word of God; praying always with all prayer and supplication in the Spirit, being watchful to this end with all perseverance and supplication for all the saints. . ."*
> (Ephesians 6:14-18a)

I didn't waste any time. I started suiting up to make myself ready for the mission we have been given as servants of our Lord in these last days. How can we possibly expect to stand alone against the enemy without His help or the armor He has given us? Every day, we must be vigilant to wear the armor and stand watch against the enemy's weapons. We are at war, but the victory is certain! We must never forget that God has given us what we need to limit the damage, protect others, and survive the attacks of the enemy. Don't go to war unarmed and unprepared. God will be with you and the Holy Spirit will set up a standard against the enemy. You are called to stand with Him alongside that standard.

I pray that the Lord will give you the anointing of the sons of Issachar; to have wisdom to understand the times and to know what you and your church should do. I pray that the Lord will provide all you need to stand in these last days. I pray that He will give you the courage to remain standing to the end. Amen!

_____

DAY 36

POWER HOUSES AND PRAYER HOUSES

As I awoke this morning, I was aware that I had a prophetic dream during the night, but I couldn't recall any of the details. I assumed that the Lord would reveal it to me in the appropriate time as I continued to pray for wisdom and revelation. During my worship time, the Lord gave me an awesome vision of a huge building project being carried out in many nations. Buildings were being constructed in all of these different areas. As I wrote this down, I suddenly remembered the dream. The dream and the vision were the same.

I observed the construction of these buildings in something like time-lapsed photography. I saw a scene in detail and then moved forward in time to see the next phase of construction followed by another fast forward. This occurred so that I was able to see some of the buildings completed. At first, I thought the buildings were commercial buildings or perhaps large churches, because the wiring for the buildings was of a very heavy gage like those used in major commercial construction projects. The wires, circuit breakers, connections, and outlets were very large and capable of heavy duty electrical service. As the buildings neared completion, I saw that they were actually houses with extremely large living rooms to accommodate many guests at the same time. Then the Lord told me that He is calling many back to the worship styles of the first century. Meetings will more often be in homes and houses of prayer.

Having participated in home churches, this idea was fascinating. One of the challenges for small groups in homes is that they have very little power to bring about major changes or reach very many people. Then the Lord said, "Wait until I turn on the power! When my power surges through these gathering places, the world will change."

Then I saw people with suitcases arriving from various places around the world. Each explained where they came from and why they were relocating to these places. Some were missionaries who had been called from different areas of service. Some were outreach ministries called to relocate to where the power is being released. All of these people were committed to being Holy Spirit led, and readily moved wherever the Lord sent them. They were excited and smiled with expectation at what the Lord was about to do. They were like pioneers who journey out into uncharted territory at the promise of the Lord to give them new lives and prosperity in a different land. Their courage and energy was awe inspiring, and I began to imagine what the Lord could do with a group of disciples like these.

These are times which require us to be prepared to relocate, and to be geographically positioned where the Lord will release great power to those who will boldly proclaim the gospel of the kingdom. These are times when the truly committed are so filled with expectancy that their greatest concern is to be where the "glory of God" is breaking out. They are not root bound. They are not tied to houses, jobs, or comfort zones. They are 100% sold out to Jesus Christ, and ready to do whatever He commands.

As I looked at them, I wanted to be one of them. I felt energy and enthusiasm surge through my spirit, soul, and body. I'm ready Lord! Use me! How about you? Do you feel a kindred spirit with these brave pioneers of the kingdom? Do you feel the Holy Spirit urging your spirit with a call to renewed service wherever that may take you – even if it means staying where you are and starting to build a house of prayer?

This morning, I felt a double wake-up call (from the dream and from the vision). I pray that even now the Holy Spirit is moving in you to energize you for what is to come. I pray that you are ready for that surge when He turns on the power. I can't wait to see it, feel it, and be moved by it! How about you? Amen?

DAY 37

HAVING THE HEART OF JESUS

This morning, I saw the Lord, Jesus standing amidst the clouds of heaven looking down on His creation — earth and all those who live on it. I felt such a heavy weightiness in my heart. I felt His deep sadness as He watched angry, hate filled people hurting and killing one another. He was seeing every act of hatred, violence, terror, abuse, judgment, condemnation, and rage. I wondered how a heart of perfect love could stand to watch His own creation behave in such violent and evil ways. The burden was so heavy! I knew that I was only feeling a small portion of that pain, but it was almost too much to bear. I remembered a very sad verse in Ezekiel 22:30, "*So I sought for a man among them who would make a wall, and stand in the gap before Me on behalf of the land, that I should not destroy it; but I found no one.*"

I have been praying earnestly for the last few months to have the heart of Jesus. I want to love what He loves and feel what He feels toward all the people on the earth. I don't think I realized how much of a burden could accompany the feelings of love toward others. I reflected on Jeremiah 5:1, "*Run to and fro through the streets of Jerusalem; see now and know; and seek in her open places if you can find a man, if there is anyone who executes judgment, who seeks the truth, and I will pardon her.*" This morning, I felt some of the sadness behind these words from our Lord. As I looked closely at His face and posture, I felt a small part of His burden and it was almost overwhelming. I knew that I couldn't handle all of His heart and what He had to endure.

Just when the burden and pain of this was almost too much for me, something else swept over Him and me. He was looking at His bride, and great feelings of love welled up in His heart. He looked at His beloved and joy replaced some of the sadness. Yet, this too was a burden. He turned to me and said, "It has been almost two thousand years! I have been waiting for my bride to be prepared. I have provided the wedding garments, the fragrant oils, the jewels, but she still hasn't prepared herself. I have sent many messages about my plan to return soon, and have asked her over and over to prepare for the wedding feast in the kingdom. But, she is still not ready. She is still operating in so much of the fear of man, and is still hesitant to come into her fullness. I want to help her, but she is hesitant to receive and use my gifts!"

I then remembered another verse: 2 Chronicles 16:9a, "*For the eyes of the LORD run to and fro throughout the whole earth, to show Himself strong on behalf of those whose heart is loyal to Him.*" Why should we continue to fear man when the Lord is already showing Himself strong on our behalf? Oh, that we might all have hearts that are more loyal to Him! Oh, that we might conquer fear by having absolute faith in Him! Oh, that we might have the heart of David, to allow the Lord to strengthen us and train our arms for the warfare coming before His return!

I had actually been praying for only one part of His heart. I want the love! I want the grace! I want the forgiveness! I want the joy! I want the peace! But, do I want the burden? Can I handle the pain? Obviously, I cannot do it unless He comes to show Himself strong on my behalf. So, what shall I do? I resolved to pray for all of the heart of Jesus I can handle today. I pray that tomorrow, with His help, I can handle more. What is your prayer today?

113

DAY 38

HEAVEN'S DUTY FREE SHOP

This morning, the Lord blessed me with extra sleep filled with many dreams of ministry. Our Lord can give us blessings and train us up even while we sleep. What an awesome God! My morning Bible studies were very long and filled with wonderful insights from the Lord. I was so focused on my love for my Lord that I spent extra time in worship, praise, and prayer this morning. I was being blessed in so many ways, but I was slower than usual getting face down to pray for what heaven is saying today. When I did, I had what I thought was a very strange vision.

I saw a worship center filled with chairs where many people could come to spend time with the Lord. This was very normal, but as my eyes looked to the front where the worship team would normally be, I saw a brightly lit sign which read, "Duty Free Shop." There were many glass shelves filled with bottles of various colored liquids arranged to attract the eyes of would be shoppers. The shop was filled with a wide variety of items and I felt an attraction to look closer at the things available. I saw bottles of expensive perfume, scented oils, wines, and sweet delicacies.

In my mind I wondered. "What can this possibly mean?" Perhaps, this was not from the Lord. So, I asked the Holy Spirit to remove it from my mind if it was not from the Lord. Instead of going away, it came back two more times. So, I prayed again and asked the Holy Spirit for guidance. I asked if we were supposed to open worship centers in airports. I asked if we were being called to pray for travelers in the air today. I asked if we were to open prayer rooms in the airports. There was no answer to any of these requests. So, I prayed, "Holy Spirit, I just don't get it. What are you trying to tell me in this vision? Please help me to understand it. What does it mean?"

Then I heard the Holy Spirit say, "Why are you thinking in the natural in a vision from heaven?" Now that was a good question, and it put me under conviction. So I prayed again for guidance. The Lord said, "This is the duty free shop in the storehouse of heaven! It is not only duty free, but it is totally free. Come and buy without money.

> *"Ho! Everyone who thirsts, come to the waters; and you who have no money, come, buy and eat. Yes, come, buy wine and milk without money and without price. Why do you spend money for what is not bread, and your wages for what does not satisfy? Listen carefully to Me, and eat what is good, and let your soul delight itself in abundance."* (Isaiah 55:1-2)

There are oils for anointing the sick for healing. There are fragrant oils to anoint others for ministry. There are other oils to impart gifts, wisdom, and revelation. There are bottles of the new wine of the kingdom of God which you can buy without money. There are sweet delicacies from heaven – food for angels that will not only taste good, but nourish you in spirit, soul, and body." Malachi 3:10b, " *And try Me now in this,"* *says the Lord of hosts, "If I will not open for you the windows of heaven and pour out for you such blessing that there will not be room enough to receive it."*

With that word everything shifted in my mind. As we gather to worship and praise the Lord, shouldn't we expect an open heaven? Shouldn't we expect that the storehouse of heaven will be more beautiful than anything offered in this world? Shouldn't we expect that the things of the Lord will truly offer all those things that are falsely promised in fleshly advertising? Shouldn't we expect that we can reach out and take the things we need to bless us, our families, and all those we are call to minister too? Shouldn't we have a higher expectancy than we have experienced so far? Shouldn't we in faith believe that, *"Every good gift and every perfect gift is from above, and comes down from the Father of lights, with whom there is no variation or shadow of turning."* (James 1:17)

May you experience an open heaven today and always! May the duty free and cost free storehouse of God be opened for you! May you reach out in faith and take what you need! May this and every day be a day to bless the Lord for all the good things He bestows on you! *"Bless the Lord, O my soul; and all that is within me, bless His holy name! Bless the Lord, O my soul, and forget not all His benefits*: (Psalm 103:1-2)

DAY 39

DON'T BREAK YOUR VOWS

This morning during praise and worship, I was face down on the floor when I heard, "Let your 'Yes' be 'Yes' and your 'No' be 'No'. Don't break your promises to the Holy Spirit." After a time of silence, I began to examine if that was from me or from the Lord. We have experienced several times lately people saying they were coming to visit. We have purchased food and made preparations only to find out at the last moment that they were not coming. Others have told us that they are going to support some part of our ministry, but then have failed to follow through. This morning, I had not been thinking about these things, but I still wondered if that was coming from somewhere in me even though it had not been in my conscious mind. So, I prayed about it. I asked the Holy Spirit if that was from inside me or if it was from the Lord. I cried out to know what heaven is saying today; to know what would please the Lord; and to know what would please our Father God.

I was suddenly taken up into the presence of the Lord. And, I heard Him saying, "Let your 'Yes' be 'Yes' and your 'No' be 'No'. Don't make vows that you don't keep." I was reminded by the Spirit of the words of Jesus recorded in Matthew 5:37, *"But let your 'Yes' be 'Yes,' and your 'No,' 'No.' For whatever is more than these is from the evil one."* I also looked at James 5:12, *"But above all, my brethren, do not swear, either by heaven or by earth or with any other oath. But let your "Yes" be "Yes," and your "No," "No," lest you fall into judgment."* This is more serious than many of us have thought.

Then the Lord reminded me of the importance God gave to vows in the Bible. There are at least 30 references to vows, and all of them speak of the importance of keeping vows. In this present age we have lost awareness of the values surrounding the keeping of vows. I was reminded of what happened to Ananias and Sapphira, when they failed to fulfill their vow to the Holy Spirit. I was reminded of the importance Paul placed on keeping vows in His writings.

Then the Lord told me that we are in a time when integrity is critically important. We are living in a season of the last days when the church has been maligned because of leaders and people who have not kept their vows to the Lord. In Psalm 50:14, Asaph gives a word from the Lord, *"Offer to God thanksgiving, and pay your vows to the Most High."* In Psalm 56:12, David says, *"Vows made to You are binding upon me, O God; I will render praises to You,"* Solomon took the teaching of his father, David, even further in Proverbs 20:25, *"It is a snare for a man to devote rashly something as holy, and afterward to reconsider his vows."* The father taught the son, and both understood this value. A further truth is that even if our earthly fathers have not taught us these values, they are still true, and we need to rekindle the fires of integrity in our time.

Today, I asked for a message for you as well as for me, and this is what the Lord gave me. I was placed under conviction by these words. I pray that the Lord will guide you in wisdom as you consider what this means in your life and ministry. May the Lord bless you with wisdom, understanding, counsel, and guidance so that at all times you may be pleasing to Him and a blessing to His Holy Spirit! Amen!

DAY 40

PREPARING FOR HIS ARRIVAL

This morning I had a reminder of the season we are in according to the Lord's calendar. Between the Feast of Trumpets and Yom Kippur is a ten day period of repentance and preparation for judgment on the Day of Atonement. It is a great reminder of how important it is to be prepared at all times for Jesus' second coming – when He comes to reign on earth for a thousand years. Using marriage as a metaphor for the church Paul wrote in Ephesians 5:25-27, *"Husbands, love your wives, just as Christ loved the church and gave himself up for her to make her holy, cleansing her by the washing with water through the word, and to present her to himself as a radiant church, without stain or wrinkle or any other blemish, but holy and blameless."* We are living in a period of great grace to give us time to prepare the church as the radiant bride of Christ, without any stains or blemishes.

What the Lord showed to me in a vision this morning was the triumphant entry of Jesus Christ which ushered in His reign on earth. The streets were packed with adoring, cheering worshippers. This time He did not come on a lowly donkey, but on a huge royal throne. He was high and lifted up on the throne in power and great glory. All the people were so excited to see Him, welcome Him, and to be close to Him. I wanted to be in that crowd, and I was overwhelmed with a deep desire to be focused on making myself ready NOW so I can participate THEN. For too long, we have lived as if this event is far into the future and we have plenty of time to get ready. However, Jesus continually advised His followers to be ready, now.

"Watch therefore, for you do not know what hour your Lord is coming. But know this, that if the master of the house had known what hour the thief would come, he would have watched and not allowed his house to be broken into. Therefore you also be ready, for the Son of Man is coming at an hour you do not expect." (Matthew 24:42-44)

The very sign Jesus gave us of His imminent return is the lack of expectation and readiness. So, this could be the day. This could be the hour. Don't miss it! Mark 13:35-37, *"Watch therefore, for you do not know when the master of the house is coming—in the evening, at midnight, at the crowing of the rooster, or in the morning—lest, coming suddenly, he find you sleeping. And what I say to you, I say to all: Watch!"*

As the throne moved through the streets, angels were throwing something like candy to the people in the crowd. I didn't think that this was actually candy, but it represented something else – something much more precious. Then I remembered the words of Ephesians 4:7-8, *"But to each one of us grace was given according to the measure of Christ's gift. Therefore He says: "When He ascended on high, He led captivity captive, and gave gifts to men."* The precious gift being liberally given to all those who follow Christ is grace. It is the grace that saves and the grace that results in thanksgiving and praise. 2 Corinthians 4:15 (NIV), *"All this is for your benefit, so that the grace that is reaching more and more people may cause thanksgiving to overflow to the glory of God."* This is the grace that gives glory to Father God as we honor His Son for this surpassingly great gift.

The more I reflected on this vision of the coming glory of Christ as He returns to dwell on earth, the more my heart longed to be a part of that great procession of those totally committed to the Lord and making ready His return. I pray that together we will make wise use of the time and grace God has given us. I pray that we will long for His return with a deep desire to be part of the great procession of those who welcome Him back to the world He created and redeemed at such great cost. Let us not wait. Let us be in preparation now. May we be ready today! Revelation 22:20-21: *"He who testifies to these things says, 'Surely I am coming quickly.' Amen. Even so, come, Lord Jesus!" The grace of our Lord Jesus Christ be with you all. Amen."*

DAY 41

FIRST ARRIVALS IN HEAVEN

T his morning, the Lord led me to the place in heaven where the new arrivals are welcomed. The adults seemed dazed, somewhat confused, and very humbled to see where they were. The children were excited and filled with joy and wonder. It reminded me of what Jesus said, *"And he said: 'I tell you the truth, unless you change and become like little children, you will never enter the kingdom of heaven. Therefore, whoever humbles himself like this child is the greatest in the kingdom of heaven.'"* (Matthew 18:3-4) The children were ready and quickly adapted. The adults seemed to be going through a difficult transition in being made fit for heaven.

I noticed that the adults were not wearing clothes. All of the earthly symbols of success and position in life had been left behind. In this world, we have been taught to work our way to the top; to be number one; and to wear the symbols of our success proudly. This may work for the world, but it doesn't mean anything in heaven. Everyone was humbled in the presence of the Lord. They brought nothing with them to speak of their worthiness. In my mind, I knew that they were waiting to be outfitted with a garment of humbleness which would empower them to fully praise the Lord for accomplishing everything needed for them to be in the presence of the Father for eternity.

Everyone was bowing in the presence of the Lord, and no one presumed to speak, question, or request anything. For some the bowing seemed very unnatural as if this was the first time they had really known what it meant to bow before the King of kings and Lord of lords. For others this seemed very natural as if it marked a lifetime of humble obedience to the Lord. Those

122

who felt so natural before the Lord were quickly processed and moved on with the children.

Those who seemed unaccustomed to bowing were not making any visible progress with the transition, and I wondered in my heart if they had been through the judgment yet. It seemed odd that they would be here without having learned to be humble before the Lord on earth. I did not make a judgment and I did not hear an answer from the Lord about this. One thing I know is that the Lord is more gracious, loving and forgiving than I have ever fully grasped. I trusted His judgment and made none of my own.

This was a stark reminder of our need to be prepared now. We don't know when we will meet the Lord. By the wide variety of ages of those who were there, it seemed clear that we could find ourselves there at any moment in time. I felt a great desire welling up inside me to hold fast to Jesus Christ and to the victory He won for me. I felt a strong desire to humble myself before Him now so that it will be very natural on that day. I desired to wear the garment of humility and praise now so that it will be completely natural when I stand before Him. I am so thankful for Jesus! I am so thankful that I don't have to stand before Him on my own merit! I am so thankful that God has attributed the righteousness of Jesus to you and me because we have placed our faith and trust in Him and have chosen a life of obedient service.

I pray that this will be a blessing to you today! May you know Him in humble obedience and love now and forever! Amen! It just occurred to me that this happened on "Thirsty Thursday." How appropriate that the Lord would remind me of my thirst for His righteousness on this day. The Lord is so good to keep reminding us so that we can always be ready and waiting for His return.

DAY 42

THE GREAT WHITE THRONE

This morning, I was immediately taken up to the throne room where the Lord was being worshipped in great power and glory. In that place, we were all aware of the concerns on the Father's heart. He was paying close attention to people on earth and we could see each person as He watched over them. There were rich people in limousines, workers in factories, and people working on farms. The focus of the Lord was across the nations and the variety of ethnic origins was clear on the faces of the people we saw. Most of the people were going about their business completely unaware of God or that He was aware of them. This experience reminded me of Job referring to God as *"O watcher of men."* (Job 7:20) Our Father in heaven has not forgotten us and nothing about us goes unnoticed. That is good news for some and bad news for others.

I had prayed moments before to see what God was doing, feel what God was feeling, and hear what God was saying so that I could do, feel, and say the same things. Now, I was literally feeling what God was feeling toward these people who were living their lives unaware of Him. His heart was heavy with love and concern. He wanted so much more for them. He felt an agony greater than that felt by a parent whose child has rejected and abandoned them. He was not angry. He did not desire to harm or punish them. He wanted them back, because of His deep love for them.

Then I was taken in the spirit by the Holy Spirit to what looked like an isolated mountain range. The light gave the impression of a pre-dawn moment when the barren rocks of the mountain face looked like giant stone blocks serving as an impenetrable barrier. But, just as this thought went through my mind, an absolutely huge waterfall appeared in front of me with a flow of water greater than Niagara Falls. I heard the Lord say, "I am releasing a new and greater flow of living water to flood the land! I am releasing enough to fill every soul on earth to overflow!" I remembered the words of Jesus in John 7:37-38, *"On the last day, that great day of the feast, Jesus stood and cried out, saying, "If anyone thirsts, let him come to Me and drink. He who believes in Me, as the Scripture has said, out of his heart will flow rivers of living water."* As I watched this massive flow of water, I knew I was seeing the true source of the rivers spoken of by Jesus in this passage.

As I continued to watch in awe, my eyes moved heavenward. The waterfall did not begin at the top of the mountains as I first thought. It was flowing down from heaven. As I lifted my eyes higher and higher, I began to get a glimpse of the top of the falls. Just above the falls was a great white throne, and the Lord was seated on the throne. The vision of Revelation 22:1-2 (NIV) immediately came into my mind, *"Then the angel showed me the river of the water of life, as clear as crystal, flowing from the throne of God and of the Lamb down the middle of the great street of the city. On each side of the river stood the tree of life, bearing twelve crops of fruit, yielding its fruit every month. And the leaves of the tree are for the healing of the nations."*

I was led to Psalm 46:4, *"There is a river whose streams make glad the city of God, the holy place where the Most High dwells."* Then, I was reminded by the Holy Spirit that at sundown today Yom Kippur (Day of Atonement) begins. This appointed time of the Lord is a great rehearsal for the day of the White Throne Judgment. For many this will be a day of final judgment, and they will face this day with fear and trembling. But for those who are in Christ Jesus, this will be a day of the fulfillment of a great promise to enter His rest where we can drink forever from the river of living water; eat of the fruit of the Tree of Life; and live forever with our loving heavenly Father. What an awesome picture of God! Life is flowing forth from Him to bring healing, health, and eternal life to all His children!

Yom Kippur is a day to stand before the Lord in His kingdom. I pray that you will experience His presence on this awesome day! I pray that you will have a visit to the Throne Room of Heaven on this day. I pray that you will have a great visitation from the Lord that will change and define your life for all eternity. I pray that on this day, you will get a vision from God for your future that will bless you beyond all you have ever asked or imagined. I pray these things in the awesome and glorious name of Yeshua ha Messiach! Amen!!!!!

DAY 43

OAKS OF RIGHTEOUSNESS

I pray that this Yom Kippur (Day of Atonement) is filled with blessing and joy, and that you are having experiences of heavenly visitation. I also pray that you will visit the Father in His heavenly kingdom, today. This appointed time of the Lord is turning out to be very special for us. We have been surrounded by angels that we have seen, felt, and heard walking around us in our worship room. I have discerned the sweet fragrance of Jesus over and over. The presence of the Holy Spirit has been so strong that the power of His presence has been like a powerful force field that is unusually tangible. We have felt the weighty presence over us and around us since sundown last night and expect it to continue throughout this day.

This morning, I was taken up to heaven and shown so many amazing things and the surpassing glory of His presence. The scenes and visions I saw in heaven were in HD and filled with revelation and glory. At one point, I found myself standing in a forest of trees that were so large that I felt like an ant or grasshopper in comparison. I heard the Lord saying, "I am looking for oaks of righteousness to stand in my strength in this time. These trees represent those who have stood for me in the past. Now, I need more like them who are willing to pay the price to take a stand for the kingdom of God."

When Jesus quoted Isaiah 61, He stated that He was anointed to accomplish certain things. Among those accomplishments will be: *"They will be called oaks of righteousness, a planting of the LORD for the display of his splendor. They will rebuild the ancient ruins and restore the places long devastated; they will renew the ruined cities that have been devastated for generations.*" (Isaiah 61:3b-4, NIV) The trees here were representative of those who have already received this anointing from the Lord as well as those who will receive it today and in the future. But, who is willing to pay the price to take that kind of powerful stand? I pray that He will find us ready and willing to accept His calling.

As I reflected on this challenge, I found myself in the wilderness stronghold of David looking to the rugged, rocking mountains. In my spirit, I remembered the words of Psalm 121 (a song of ascent) which I believe was likely the cry of David from this wilderness place, *"I will lift up my eyes to the hills—from whence comes my help? My help comes from the* LORD, *Who made heaven and earth. He will not allow your foot to be moved; He who keeps you will not slumber. Behold, He who keeps Israel shall neither slumber nor sleep." The* LORD *is your keeper; the* LORD *is your shade at your right hand. The sun shall not strike you by day, nor the moon by night. The* LORD *shall preserve you from all evil; He shall preserve your soul. The* LORD *shall preserve your going out and your coming in from this time forth, and even forevermore."*

We are living in a day of great fear. People tremble and withdraw from a harsh stare or a judgmental glance. People get offended and desert the ranks over small offenses. Where will we find people who will stand for the Lord like the mighty oaks of righteousness? Where will we find people like Isaiah described, *"Because the Sovereign LORD helps me, I will not be disgraced. Therefore have I set my face like flint, and I know I will not be put to shame."* (Isaiah 50:7, NIV) We need some courageous believers who will fix their faces like flint and not back down from their faith in the Lord. But, where will He find them? Will He find any amongst us?

Today is an appointed time to reflect on the Lord's great Day of Judgment. How will that day be for us? As I reflect on this rehearsal for that day, I am so thankful for Jesus. I am so thankful that I will be judged by what He did and not on my own works and merit! I am so thankful that this is a day of redemption and not a day of judgment and condemnation. I stand convicted that my gratitude must result in commitment. My praise must result in obedience. My worship must result in a faith that will not let go of what God has placed in my hands and heart. I want to be an oak of righteousness. How about you?

May the Lord bless you with a deep understanding and revelation of His purposes in your life! May the calling of the Lord lay claim to your heart and service as you fix your face like flint! May you never be ashamed of Him, and may your shame which He bore on the cross never return to your spirit! May you be an oak of righteousness, a planting of the Lord! Amen!

DAY 44

FALLING SCROLLS

Last year, I continuously saw great clouds turning counterclockwise as I heard the Lord declaring a season of
restoration. True to His Word, He restored so many things
in the lives of His people. Many even began to look and act
younger as their appearance seemed to be turned back to an
earlier age. Sons and daughters were restored to waiting parents. Ministries were restored to those who had been rejected
by rebellious people.

However, this morning, a great storm cloud that was larger
than the earth itself, was overhead rotating in a clockwise direction. And I heard the Lord saying, "The time is advancing! I am
moving things ahead rapidly! This is a year for moving ahead
at ever increasing speed." As the new year of the Lord was
ushered in on Rosh Hashanah, we moved into a new season.
This is the spiritual year of the Lion of the Tribe of Judah who
is roaring into the earth causing things around the globe to be
shaken. The old things have passed away and all things are
new. Are we able to adapt to new seasons in the Lord?

As I watched the great storm cloud turn, scrolls began to fall
from it toward earth. There were several types of scrolls and
all were huge. Some were written on both sides like the scroll
seen by Ezekiel, *"Then I looked, and I saw a hand stretched
out to me. In it was a scroll, which he unrolled before me. On
both sides of it were written words of lament and mourning and
woe."* (Ezekiel 2:9-10, NIV) These scrolls reminded me of the
one in Revelation 5:1, *"Then I saw in the right hand of him who
sat on the throne a scroll with writing on both sides and sealed
with seven seals."* It was made clear to me that warnings of

130

judgment were being released as an act of grace so that God's obedient servants may repent and be prepared.

Other scrolls seemed to be on fire but not being consumed. The fire was the glory of the Lord, and He was releasing this to faithful people and faithful ministries to set them on fire for this season of preparation for judgment. These scrolls were much larger than the judgment scrolls making it clear that the glory of God is the goodness of God. His grace is always sufficient. His grace is always greater that His desire for justice. His mercy is from everlasting to everlasting! Amen! Thanks be to our Lord, Jesus Christ, who has made this possible!

As I watched in awe, watches and clocks began to fall from the storm cloud. The watches came gently upon the heads of God's people and were absorbed into each head. The Lord said, "I am releasing an awareness of the times into those who are obedient and faithful to do what I say! These will have an increased awareness of the closeness of my coming!" I felt a slight concern for the clocks falling. I thought they might be hitting people on the head to give them a wakeup call. However, the clocks fell on churches where they were to help congregations become more aware of the season that is approaching.

All of this, I had observed in a night sky. But, at this point, I saw the sun beginning to break forth over the horizon with greater and greater brightness and glory. Suddenly the sun was clearly visible, and came up with a blazing white brilliance. Thank God that our spiritual eyes can look into the sun without damage. As I continue to look in awe, I heard the Lord saying, "The sun is rising! The Son is rising! The night has passed, and now the Son is coming!"

My thoughts immediately were on you, and I prayed: "Lord, may you know the times and seasons! May you be fully ready for that day! May you be making all your spiritual preparations for the day of His appearing! May you be watching, waiting, and ready for His times and seasons! May you be filled with an urgency to call others to get ready for the coming of the Lord! Amen!

DAY 45

SIGNS AND WONDERS

oday the awesome weighty presence of the Lord is as strong or perhaps stronger than it was on Yom Kippur. We continue to experience angelic presence and the power of the Holy Spirit. As we approach Sukkot (Feast of Tabernacles), the mighty presence of the Lord continues to come in greater power. This year, as we meet the Lord at His appointed time and rehearse the coming day when He will dwell with us in fullness, may you experience all the mighty signs and wonders He has in store for you!

This morning, the Lord again gave me a series of visions. I will share two with you in this message. First, I saw an elderly woman dressed in a heavy winter coat who was standing before the Lord in the spirit. As I watched her, she began to rise above the ground and float in the air. The meaning of this was not clear to me. So, I asked the Holy Spirit to help me understand it. The Holy Spirit said, "Ancient promises are soon to be fulfilled. Things you have been waiting for a long time are about to be manifest. You are soon to entered into the fullness of the promise in Joel 2:28-31, *"And it shall come to pass afterward that I will pour out My Spirit on all flesh; your sons and your daughters shall prophesy, your old men shall dream dreams, your young men shall see visions. And also on My menservants and on My maidservants I will pour out My Spirit in those days. And I will show wonders in the heavens and in the earth: Blood and fire and pillars of smoke. The sun shall be turned into darkness, and the moon into blood, before the coming of the great and awesome day of the Lord."* (to understand the full impact of this promise, it is essential to study verse 1 through verse 27)

The focal point of the vision was actually on verse 30, "*And I will show wonders in the heavens and in the earth: blood and fire and pillars of smoke.*" The rising of the woman was pointing to the coming time when we will all see wonders in heaven and signs on the earth. So often we have focused on the gifts of the Spirit and more specifically the release of prophetic gifts on people of all ages, gender, and nationality. However, in this season, expect to see the signs and wonders displayed in the heavens and on the earth.

As I reflected on this, I was carried in the Spirit to a different place. In this vision, I was traveling on a super highway. There were no apparent exits from the highway, but many entrances. At each of these entrances, large commercial freight trucks were merging into traffic. The flow of traffic became heavier and heavier with each new arrival on the roadway. I asked the Holy Spirit to guide me to understand this vision. The Lord said, "I am opening a highway of holiness for my people to travel in this season of signs and wonders. And, there will be more than ample provision for all who travel with me. An abundance of supply is being released all along this highway to bless and sustain all my people who travel with me." I went to Isaiah 35, and found all of this clearly prophesied there.

> "*Then the eyes of the blind shall be opened, and the ears of the deaf shall be unstopped. Then the lame shall leap like a deer, and the tongue of the dumb sing. For waters shall burst forth in the wilderness, and streams in the desert. The parched ground shall become a pool, and the thirsty land springs of water; In the habitation of jackals, where each lay, there shall be grass with reeds and rushes. A highway shall be there,*

and a road, and it shall be called the Highway of Holiness." (Isaiah 35:5-8)

The ancient promises are being fulfilled and the things hoped for are now manifesting. What an awesome day. In addition to the wonders in the sky, we are going to see a greater release of the power gifts of the Holy Spirit. We are entering into an era when gifts of healings and working of miracles will again be common place among those led by the Holy Spirit. Dry places in the wilderness of our souls will become fruitful and filled with life once again. Begin now to pray and prepare so that you will experience the fullness that the Lord has prepared for you! Time is short! The day of His appearing is at hand. I see this in the nearness of the celebration of Sukkot. It is so close. Be ready! Be watchful! Be prepared to move into a new reality of His presence! Expect wonders in the heavens and signs on the earth! *"Therefore I remind you to stir up the gift of God which is in you through the laying on of my hands."* (2 Timothy 1:6) Amen!!!! Even so, come quickly, Lord Jesus!

———————————

DAY 46

A LIVING WATER FLOOD

I pray that in this special season of the Lord, that you are experiencing His weighty presence as you give him wholehearted worship and praise. We continue to feel His presence strongly as we are also experiencing angelic visitation on a daily basis. Remember, tomorrow at sundown the Feast of Tabernacles begins. As we meet with the Lord at His appointed time and rehearse for the day that He will dwell with us for a thousand years, excitement should be building because even now He lives in us and we live in Him. What an amazing and awesome Father God whose goodness is His glory!

This morning I again had a series of interrelated visions. As I prayed for the Holy Spirit to tell me what heaven is saying today, I was carried in the spirit to a place where people were gathering to worship the Lord. Even though this place seemed to be in heaven, it was a scene typical of most churches as people gather for worship. There was a low hum of many voices greeting others, catching up on news, and sharing family stories. Some were moving to areas of the church where they enjoyed standing or sitting during the time of worship. As this scene unfolded, a woman walked up to my wife, Gloria, and handed her a partially filled bottle of water as she asked, "Would you hold this for me? I don't want anything to distract me from worship. And I don't want to do anything which might cause me to displease the Lord?" As she returned to her place, I thought, "Now that's odd! She didn't want anything that would distract her or displease the Lord, but she didn't mind asking someone else to do it in her place." So, I prayed,

"Holy Spirit, I am going to need some help with this one. What does this mean?"

I heard the Lord saying, "I promised you rivers of living water flowing out of your heart, but many have tried to bottle it up so they can control it and limit the flow. They want to pick and choose when and where to let it flow. Some want to bottle it and make an idol of it. Some want to bottle it and use it for their own purposes. When this happens it will distract them and it will interfere with their relationship to the Father." I remembered once again His proclamation in John 7:37-38, *"On the last day, that great day of the feast, Jesus stood and cried out, saying, "If anyone thirsts, let him come to Me and drink. He who believes in Me, as the Scripture has said, out of his heart will flow rivers of living water."*

As I meditated on this word, I was quickly carried to a raging river which had already gone beyond flood stage. I watched as people gathered behind a solid barrier which protected them from the main flow of the river. Even though protected from the swift water, they were still being pounded by waves repeatedly striking against the barrier. Each was holding on for dear life as the river raged around them. The Lord said, "It is this fear which prevents many from experiencing the river of living water. They fear that it will sweep them away or overwhelm them with its power. So, they look for places to hide where they can attempt to limit the flow. But, this is not a true image of the river flowing from the heart. The enemy is the source of this fear." I remembered Romans 10:17, *"So then faith comes by hearing, and hearing by the word of God."* I have always believed that fear comes by hearing as well. It comes by hearing the words of the enemy. The enemy does not want you to have living waters flowing out of your heart into others who may be enlivened and freed from bondage to him.

Jesus said, *"Brood of vipers! How can you, being evil, speak good things? For out of the abundance of the heart the mouth speaks. A good man out of the good treasure of his heart brings forth good things, and an evil man out of the evil treasure brings forth evil things.*" (Matthew 12:34-35) If the abundance of your heart is living water, then living water will flow forth and your mouth will continuously speak it into the lives of others. We need to embrace the flow of living water rather than attempting to bottle it up, control it, or hide from it. We need to trust our Father God that he will bless us with the river rather than overwhelm or hurt us.

May you be faith filled! May you have rivers of living water flowing forth from your heart! May you trust the Lord and enjoy what He is doing with your life and the lives of others you bless! May the words of your mouth carry living water which will produce fruit worthy of the kingdom of God! Amen!

DAY 47

CALENDARS ARE AGREEING

W e are living in an amazing time when our calendars are coming together in agreement to open the door for us to worship and praise our great God and the Father of our Lord, Jesus Christ. Today, Korea celebrated their traditional day of thanksgiving while in Israel today at sundown the Lord's appointed time of Sukkot begins. Sukkot is truly an appointed time for all nations to meet with the Lord and celebrate His dwelling with Israel in the wilderness; His dwelling in our hearts right now through Christ; and His future plan to dwell with us forever as our Father God. We have so much to be thankful for today and always. Praise the Lord, O my Soul, and all that is within me praise His holy Name! Amen!

All morning, the Lord has been giving me visions of pre-dawn scenes around the world. Each was beautiful and I was enjoying my experience, but I didn't immediately understand the significance of these visions. So, I asked the Holy Spirit to guide me in understanding what these scenes meant. As I finished my request, I suddenly saw the sun break forth over the horizon and flood the entire area with brilliant light. As I watched, I heard the Lord say, "Something is about to dawn on the earth! I'm getting ready to release great light on the earth that will shatter every area of darkness. I am coming to dwell with my people!" This prophecy is given in four books of the Bible. In the New Testament, Paul reissues it, *"And what agreement has the temple of God with idols? For you are the temple of the living God. As God has said: 'I will dwell in them and walk among them. I will be their God, and they shall be My people.'"* (2 Corinthians 6:16)

When God breaks forth like the dawn and comes to dwell with His people it will be for all nations on earth. Zechariah 2:10-11, *"'Sing and rejoice, O daughter of Zion! For behold, I am coming and I will dwell in your midst,' says the LORD.' Many nations shall be joined to the LORD in that day, and they shall become My people. And I will dwell in your midst. Then you will know that the LORD of hosts has sent Me to you.'"* That was the message I was being given in the pre-dawn scenes around the world. The Lord is coming to dwell with us. Hallelujah! He will be our God and we will be His people! Hallelujah!

Today, as we meet with the Lord at His appointed time, we are called upon to rehearse for that day. In the rehearsal, we continue to prepare ourselves so that we can be with Him – to rule and reign with Him for a thousand years on this earth and forever and ever in the new heaven and new earth. Amen? Hallelujah! Wow, we have so much to celebrate! But there is more good news. We don't have to wait to experience the joy of dwelling with Him. Meditate today on some of His awesome promises about dwelling with us, now:

> *"Jesus answered and said to him, 'If anyone loves Me, he will keep My word; and My Father will love him, and We will come to him and make Our home with him.'"* (John 14:23)

> *"If you abide in Me, and My words abide in you, you will ask what you desire, and it shall be done for you. By this My Father is glorified, that you bear much fruit; so you will be My disciples."* (John 15:7-8)

> *"If you keep My commandments, you will abide in My love, just as I have kept My Father's commandments and abide in His love."* (John 15:10)

"Therefore 'Come out from among them and be separate,' says the Lord. 'Do not touch what is unclean, and I will receive you. I will be a Father to you, and you shall be My sons and daughters, says the Lord Almighty.'" (2 Corinthians 6:17-18)

May you be blessed to fully experience the Lord's presence in your heart, life, family, and ministry! May you be ready now to dwell with Him forever! May this be a season of visiting with Him in the third heaven as well as in this earthly tent! May you know the joy of abiding in His love both now and forever! Amen!

DAY 48

AS A LITTLE CHILD

Wow! Almighty God, the creator of the universe, the King of kings and the Lord of lords wants to dwell with us – you and me! This is such an awesome thought! Most of us have never had a face to face with a senator, congressman, governor, or president. Yet, our Father God wants to come and live with us and in us forever and ever! Isn't that amazing and wonderful? And, He has already started by putting His Holy Spirit in us to instruct us and prepare us for this glorious reality which may come into fullness at any moment.

This morning I had an interesting visit in the Throne Room of Heaven. I was shown the faces of many children and was so impressed by the purity, innocence, and peace on their faces. These children seemed to range in age from two years old up to pre-teens. I saw very small children sitting on the floor and playing in complete ease and comfort while things were happening all around them. They were so at home and so very comfortable in the presence of the Lord. Whatever events had caused them to depart earth at such an early age seemed completely forgotten and they were at such wonderful peace.

As I watched the children with fascination and joy, I heard the Lord saying, "If you want to see my face – if you want to visit these heavenly places – if you want to dwell with me, you need to become more like these. You need to learn complete trust and faith!" As the Lord said this, I was shown a small child, perhaps two years old looking up to the Lord as He spoke with me. There before me was the perfect example of what the Lord was saying. The look on that face (we've all seen it) was a picture of complete love, trust, and confidence like a child looking up to a loving parent. I remembered the words of Jesus in Matthew 18:2-5, *"Then Jesus called a little child to Him, set him in the midst of them, and said, "Assuredly, I say to you, unless you are converted and become as little children, you will by no means enter the kingdom of heaven. Therefore whoever humbles himself as this little child is the greatest in the kingdom of heaven. Whoever receives one little child like this in My name receives Me."*

So, how do we as battle hardened warriors, set in our ways, go through a change so significant that the Lord calls it a conversion? In Romans 12:1-2, Paul describes it this way: *"I beseech you therefore, brethren, by the mercies of God, that you present your bodies a living sacrifice, holy, acceptable to God, which is your reasonable service. And do not be conformed to this world, but be transformed by the renewing of your mind, that you may prove what is that good and acceptable and perfect will of God."* The word renewing carries the idea of an ongoing process. The problem is that most people want instant and complete works. They want it all and they want it now! But to please God and be prepared for His presence, we need to be involved in an ongoing process of renewing our minds. According to Paul, those willing to do this actually prove or demonstrate the *"good and acceptable and perfect will of God."*

We need to let go of a closet full of old hurts, resentments, and un-forgiveness. We need to become pure and innocent in our minds again. For most of us that will be a lifelong process. So, let's get started now! Being in the presence of the Lord is my top priority. I don't want to hold on to anything that blocks that or prevents me from receiving all that the Holy Spirit has for me. So, I am ready and willing to be renewed and transformed. How about you? We can't have it both ways. We cannot serve two masters. If you are mastered by your emotions and old disappointments and disillusionments, you need to change masters. That old and cruel master will never get you to where you want to be. None of that old stuff compares with what God has for you. So, let it go! Choose to be rid of it (daily if necessary), and get yourself free to be with the Lord.

In this appointed time with the Lord, may you experience the fullness of the blessing as you spend time with the Lord! May you visit Him in the heavenly places where you have already been seated (Ephesians 2:6)! May you experience love, forgiveness, peace and joy as never before! May the Lord bless you and keep you forever in His loving presence! Amen!

DAY 49

ENTER INTO HIS REST

This morning I kept seeing images of people working hard, rushing from place to place, and giving their best to accomplish important things. Some had the appearance of movie stars, TV actors, and other celebrities. I thought at first that these were random images and I needed to get past them to find out what heaven is saying today. But, they continued to come. So, I just waited for the Holy Spirit to guide me.

Then I heard the Lord say, "Rest!" After a long pause, I heard Him say again, "Rest!" This happened several times, and then I heard the Lord say, "My people are still striving so hard to show themselves worthy. They are still striving so much to prove their righteousness. They are too busy doing good things to rest in me and get to know me in the depth of their hearts. Even their prayers are like hard labor as they are driven to accomplish the task of prayer and intercession in an attempt to please me. They are like Martha who was doing good things, but missed the better thing. I want more to be like Mary who knew how to spend time with me — listening and getting to know me better."

As I read Jeremiah 17 this morning, I was taken by the Word of God saying that if the people would just keep the Sabbath, the judgment spoken in the prophesy of Jeremiah would be lifted. Jeremiah 17:24-27, "'And it shall be, if you heed Me carefully,' says the Lord, 'to bring no burden through the gates of this city on the Sabbath day, but hallow the Sabbath day, to do no work in it, then shall enter the gates of this city kings and princes sitting on the throne of David, riding in chariots and on horses, they and their princes, accompanied by the men of Judah and the inhabitants of Jerusalem; and this city shall *remain forever. And they shall come from the cities of Judah and from the places around Jerusalem, from the land of Benjamin and from the lowland, from the mountains and from the South, bringing burnt offerings and sacrifices, grain offerings and incense, bringing sacrifices of praise to the house of the Lord. But if you will not heed Me to hallow the Sabbath day, such as not carrying a burden when entering the gates of Jerusalem on the Sabbath day, then I will kindle a fire in its gates, and it shall devour the palaces of Jerusalem, and it shall not be quenched.'"* As simple as this seems, people then and now go about their business without regarding the Sabbath rest. How much blessing and favor have we missed because we have not learned this one simple lesson?

After an impassioned plea for entering God's rest, the writer of Hebrews gives an awesome promise from God: *"Seeing then that we have a great High Priest who has passed through the heavens, Jesus the Son of God, let us hold fast our confession. For we do not have a High Priest who cannot sympathize with our weaknesses, but was in all points tempted as we are, yet without sin. Let us therefore come boldly to the throne of grace, that we may obtain mercy and find grace to help in time of need."* (Hebrews 4:14-16) The key point is to know the Lord well enough to come boldly before the Throne of Grace. By the way, the Throne of Grace is in the Third Heaven.

Many of you have jobs which require you to work on Saturday and you let Sunday be your Sabbath rest. Many have jobs that require the work of ministry on the Biblical Sabbath. Don't get caught up in rules. Remember Jesus' words in Mark 2:27-28, *"And He said to them, 'The Sabbath was made for man, and not man for the Sabbath. Therefore the Son of Man is also Lord of the Sabbath.'"* The point is to spend time with the Lord free from striving and laboring to be approved. We must learn to simply spend time with Him quietly listening to His voice. God is not calling us back to another form of works righteousness. He is inviting us into a deeper and more meaningful relationship with Him. To keep this relationship deep and focused on Him, we need to develop some quiet times with Him – not just quietness from outside noise, but quietness in our spirits and bodies so we can hear Him. (Talk less! Listen more!)

May you find a place and time of quiet rest with the Lord! May you grow daily in your knowledge of Him and your loving relationship with Him! May you find time to listen for His voice! Amen! Remember, His sheep know His voice and listen to Him.

DAY 50

WEDDING FEAST OF THE LAMB

This morning, I was transported in the Spirit to a very large open garden. Everything was vibrant with color. I have never seen such beautiful and deep shades of green in the grass which was spread across the entire expanse like a perfectly manicured carpet. There were huge rose bushes filled with buds and blossoms. White outdoor tables and white chairs (like wrought iron) were everywhere with a vast number of guests in formal attire. There was a very festive atmosphere in this place as we were surrounded by peace, quiet, joy, excitement, and anticipation. I was not yet aware of the purpose of this gathering, but I was very glad to be among the invited guests.

A very large white limousine slowly made its way through the crowd and came to a stop near where I was standing. I wondered what dignitary would be ushered in with this kind of honor. I watched as the door was opened by a waiting servant wearing a tuxedo and white gloves. As the door opened fully, I saw her. She was beautiful in her flowing white wedding gown. It was the bride! And I knew immediately that this was the bride of Christ arriving for the great wedding feast of the lamb. As the door opened, the entire area was filled with the aroma of her perfume and the fragrant oils she had been bathed in for a very long time. As she turned to be escorted out of the limousine by waiting servants extending white gloved hands, I was struck by the absolute whiteness of her dress. The dress and veil were blazing white and seemed to be radiating their own light. The dress was covered in beautiful white diamonds.

*"And I heard, as it were, the voice of a great mul-
titude, as the sound of many waters and as the
sound of mighty thunderings, saying, "Alleluia!
For the Lord God Omnipotent reigns! Let us be
glad and rejoice and give Him glory, for the marriage of the Lamb has come, and His wife has
made herself ready." And to her it was granted
to be arrayed in fine linen, clean and bright, for
the fine linen is the righteous acts of the saints.
Then he said to me, 'Write: Blessed are those who
are called to the marriage supper of the Lamb!'
And he said to me, 'These are the true sayings of
God.'"* (Revelation 19:6-9)

As I watched in great awe and fullness of joy, the entire
area was filled with an intensely bright light. As I took my eyes
off the bride and looked toward the light I saw Jesus riding
toward the bride on a magnificent white horse arrayed with a
gold bridle, bejeweled beyond anything I had imagined. My
eyes quickly focused on Jesus. His radiance was like the sun
blazing forth with pure white light from His robe and crown.
The glow gave an appearance that His hair had turned white,
but His youthful appearance made it clear that nothing about
Him had grown old or faded in its glory. His face was filled
with joy at the sight of His bride and you could clearly see the
pride on His face at the work of His hands standing before Him.

I was suddenly aware that other people were watching, but
they were not invited guests. The Spirit carried me to a place
where I could see them clearly. They were looking through a
glass like bubble covered with ashes and soot. Some people
had moved close to the glass. They had wiped away enough of
the black soot to see the celebration. There was great torment
on their faces. Their mouths, jaws and teeth were larger than
normal people. It was as if they had been given a form which
allowed greater weeping, wailing, and gnashing of teeth. I

heard some of their cries. Some of the things I heard spoken with great agony in their voices were: "I thought I would be there." "I thought I was good enough to be invited." "I thought I was a Christian because I prayed a prayer once."

I remembered what Jesus said in Matthew 8:12, *"But the sons of the kingdom will be cast out into outer darkness. There will be weeping and gnashing of teeth."* Did you catch that? Some of the sons and daughters of the kingdom will be in outer darkness. All those who have not properly prepared for the wedding feast will be with them in outer darkness. *"But when the king came in to see the guests, he saw a man there who did not have on a wedding garment. So he said to him, 'Friend, how did you come in here without a wedding garment?' And he was speechless. Then the king said to the servants, 'Bind him hand and foot, take him away, and cast him into outer darkness; there will be weeping and gnashing of teeth.' "For many are called, but few are chosen."* (Matthew 22:11-14)

These were especially painful and sobering words after participating in the joy and celebration of those at the wedding feast. We need to intensify our preparations for the great end time harvest. We need to help as many as possible to avoid the outer darkness. I received this vision as another wake-up call for the body of Christ. May we be busily about our Father's business when Jesus returns to take His bride home to the place He has already prepared in His Father's house! Amen?

I was so happy that the vision didn't end in outer darkness. I was transported back to the garden by the Spirit. As I looked at one of the rose buds on a large rose bush, it suddenly burst open in brilliant white and something like white fire exploded out of the bud. All of the dark petals that had surround the bud were broken off and sent flying through the air. It was clear that every dark thing that had surrounded the bud had been broken off and cast away. Every sin, failure, and broken promise had been redeemed and this rose (representing the church) was recreated into the beautiful flower God had intended. It was clear that this was not the work of the rose, but the work of Yeshua ha Messiah. It was glorious, but only the beginning. Every rosebud on every bush suddenly broke forth in brilliance and the entire area was filled with the light of His glory, holiness, and grace. Amen! Hallelujah! What an awesome Father God! What an awesome redeeming Lord who is our glorious Bridegroom forever and ever. Amen!!!!!!! Hallelujah!!!!!

DAY 51

A TIME OF REFRESHING

This morning I was carried in the spirit to a vineyard with beautiful green leaves and huge bunches of grapes hanging from the vines. In this vision, I was under the vines looking up at the grapes hanging from the vines. At first, this angle of view seemed odd, and then I remembered a vineyard I visited in Korea in 1983. The vines had been carefully guided to provide a cover over a small room with chairs and tables. As you sat under the vines, you were served freshly picked grapes. I remembered how pleasant it was to sit under the grape laden vines eating those delicious fresh grapes.

I remembered and relived that wonderful experience from my past as I sat under a similar place in the Lord's garden vineyard. As I gazed on the beautiful ripe green grapes, I heard the Lord say, "This is a place of refreshment! This is a place of replenishment! This is a place of abundant supply!" As I meditated on these words and thought of many possible meanings in these three short sentences, I was given three visions within the vision.

First, I saw an older man running and jumping around under the vines. My eyes were drawn to his knees. They were very large and strong. I understood that he had been healed of severe knee damage. Now, the knees were stronger and better than they had been before. In his excitement over this healing, he was dancing, jumping, and running vigorously around the entire area under the vines. I believe that someone is receiving a glorious healing in his or her knees right now. If this is you, just receive it and begin to move freely. Celebrate and praise God for this marvelous gift. Job 4:4, "*Your words have upheld him who was stumbling, and you have strengthened the feeble knees."*

Next, I saw a woman who was very burdened down with sadness and loss. There was a terrible spirit of depression over her and in her spirit. Her attitude seemed to be one of hopelessness. As I watched, a beautiful glass, filled with the new wine of heaven, came down from one of the clusters of grapes overhead. The color of the wine was the same as the color of the grapes. As she sipped the wine, all of the depression, sadness, and hopelessness were broken off and she was set free. Zechariah 9:16-17, *"The LORD their God will save them in that day, as the flock of His people. For they shall be like the jewels of a crown, lifted like a banner over His land—For how great is its goodness and how great its beauty! Grain shall make the young men thrive, and new wine the young women."* If this is you, just reach out and take the new wine and drink deeply as you receive your healing!

The third scene was something like a magic act on stage. I saw a sofa and coffee table under the vines. A man and a woman were sitting on the sofa. The woman had a newspaper opened in front of her covering her except for her hands holding up the paper on either side. As I watched, the newspaper fell to the floor and the woman was gone. I was shown the scene again from the side so that I could see what happened. The hands on the paper were not really her hands but part of a mechanical device to hold the paper while she disappeared. After she left, the man tripped the mechanism which caused the paper to collapse over the device which was hiding it from the view of the audience. The message was of someone who is so covered with the problems of this world that she is lost behind all the bad reports from the media. She needed to get away from all of the stress and worry of world events. Her husband helped her by covering for her as she made a getaway for a short vacation. The Lord wants to set someone free from worry about bad news and the anxiety of worldwide trouble. You need a break and the Lord is covering for you while you slip away for a time of replenishment and renewal. And the Bridegroom said, *"Come to Me, all you who labor and are heavy laden, and I will give you rest. Take My yoke upon you and learn from Me, for I am gentle and lowly in heart, and you will find rest for your souls. For My yoke is easy and My burden is light."* (Matthew 11:28-29)

In this season of refreshment, replenishment and abundant supply, the Lord has opened the resources of heaven over you. Look up and see what the Lord has done for you! Look up and see the storehouse of heaven open above you! Reach up and take a glass filled with the new wine of Heaven! Then be refreshed, replenished and supplied with all you need for you, your family, your business, your church, your ministry, or any other need you may have today! The Lord has released a season of open heaven provision. Don't miss out on your opportunity for favor and blessing! Amen!

ALL THINGS WORK FOR GOOD

T his morning in my worship time, I suddenly had a vision
in ultra HD clarity. I was standing in an old abandoned
factory which seemed to have been turned into a warehouse
before being totally abandoned. The building was in very bad
shape with lots of oily dirt, spider webs, broken windows, and
darkness in every corner. However, in front of me, one of the
machines with a vertical shaft was spinning at a very high rate
of speed in a counterclockwise direction. This machine was
well oiled, highly polished, and in excellent working order.
In the middle of the spinning shaft was a spool of material
which was either a strong fabric or some type of wire mesh.
It was spinning so fast that it was difficult to tell what the
fabric was like.

As I watched this spinning shaft, I heard the Lord say, "I
am turning all of this backward. The owners were negligent
and took this factory in the wrong direction. They didn't
understand the times and failed to adjust to the market so they
could produce the right products. They attempted to salvage
part of their investment by diversifying, but it failed because
they were still headed in the wrong direction."

After I heard the Lord say this, I was drawn to look beyond
the right side of the machine. From this perspective, I had a view
of a back room. In this room, I saw a large round table covered
in green felt. I could tell that it was a gambling table and many
games of poker had been played on this table. However, today
there were no cards on the table. On the table in front of each of
the seven chairs, I saw note pads and other kinds of papers used
to take notes. At first I thought that men had gathered to make

evil plans or attempt to save the business by continuing to go in the wrong direction. Obviously, they had turned it into a place of gambling, vice, and wickedness of all kinds. But, then I saw them! There were Bibles on the table in front of each chair next to the stacks of papers. This place which was built by the enemy for his evil purposes had been transformed by God into a place to fulfill His purposes. Then I heard the Lord say, "I am turning the tables on them!"

It was only then that I realized that there were many other gambling tables in this room. This had been some sort of underground casino where many people had indulged the desires of the flesh and sinned against God. As this thought sunk in, I heard the Lord say, "As with the machine which is spinning backward to the time when this was a kingdom business (long before it had been turned to follow the wrong way), I am turning the tables forward to a time of dedication to my will and purpose!"

I reflected on that message from the Lord. He is turning things backward and forward at the same time. That is an awesome thought. Only God would think like that. I remembered the words of Isaiah 55:8-9, "*'For My thoughts are not your thoughts, nor are your ways My ways,' says the LORD. 'For as the heavens are higher than the earth, so are My ways higher than your ways, and My thoughts than your thoughts.'*"

I was moved back in front of the machine where I watched it continue to spin. Then, I noticed for the first time that the shaft spinning backward from its intended purpose was actually spinning clockwise in God's purpose. This shaft was also turning backward and forward at the same time. We can make our plans and move in our own purposes in rebellion to God, but in the spirit realm we are still moving in God's direction. My thoughts were turned to Proverbs 19:21 (NIV), "*Many are the plans in a man's heart, but it is the Lord's purpose that prevails.*"

I meditated on this awesome thought — what people meant for evil, God meant for His good. Genesis 50:19-20 (NIV),

"But Joseph said to them, "Don't be afraid. Am I in the place of God? You intended to harm me, but God intended it for good to accomplish what is now being done, the saving of many lives." This is the perspective God wants to implant in us. To see in everything that happens (regardless of the intention of people to do evil) that God is working for our good. So, don't lose hope! No matter what people are trying to do to you, God will turn it into the good He intends for you. Trust in God and do not fear man. What can man do to those who are blessed of the Lord?

Even if a nation, city, church, family, or individual has rebelled (even for a long time) against the Lord, He is ready to restore! He is ready to turn the tables and return you to the future He has planned for you all along. Don't grow weary or give up on His purposes! He will always prevail. Remember, *"'No weapon formed against you shall prosper, and every tongue which rises against you in judgment You shall condemn. This is the heritage of the servants of the LORD, and their righteousness is from Me,' Says the LORD."* (Isaiah 54:17)

Meditate on these thoughts from the Lord. He is turning all things backward and forward at the same time. We can make our plans for the future, but His plan will prevail. In these last days, everything is moving backward and forward to the time of Messiah's return. It is a time to be thinking and seeing things God's way. Even so, come quickly Lord Jesus! Amen!

DAY 53

THE SOLE SOURCE

This morning, I heard the Lord say, "Sole Source." This brought to mind the years I spent in the military writing "sole source justifications" for everything I ordered. This was necessary so that I would get the products or services I really wanted. The substitutes were never useful or appropriate. It was so important to get the right material or the right person if you wanted the job done correctly and to standard. However, I wondered what "Sole Source" meant coming from the Lord.

Then I was shown in a vision the outside of the US Mint where all the authentic money is manufactured in the USA. I heard the Lord say, "This is the sole source for legitimate currency in the United States. All other currency which appears to be real is actually counterfeit." Then I was carried to a heavenly place where the power of God was present in a spiritual form, and I heard the Lord say, "The Holy Spirit is the sole source for spiritual gifts. All others are counterfeit. Beware in this season of the impartation of counterfeit gifts and false spirits!" 2 Corinthians 11:14-15, "*And no wonder! For Satan himself transforms himself into an angel of light. Therefore it is no great thing if his ministers also transform themselves into ministers of righteousness, whose end will be according to their works.*"

How are we to know the difference between the false and the true? John 10:1-5 (NIV), "*I tell you the truth, the man who does not enter the sheep pen by the gate, but climbs in by some other way, is a thief and a robber. The man who enters by the gate is the shepherd of his sheep. The watchman opens the gate for him, and the sheep listen to his voice. He calls his own*

158

sheep by name and leads them out. When he has brought out all his own, he goes on ahead of them, and his sheep follow him because they know his voice. But they will never follow a stranger; in fact, they will run away from him because they do not recognize a stranger's voice."

The Lord's message was clear this morning. We need to beware of false prophets and false prophecies! We need to understand that the enemy always makes counterfeits of all God's works to include prophecy! We need to get to know the real thing! We need to know the voice of our Good Shepherd so we will follow no other.

May you hear the Lord's voice today! May your spiritual eyes be opened more and more each day! May the Holy Spirit bless you with all spiritual blessings and especially the gift of discernment! May you discern more and more clearly the work of the Holy Spirit and God's ministering angels assigned to you and your ministry! Amen!

THE HEART SPEAKS

This morning, the Lord gave me visions of revival fires in Israel, Korea, and the USA. As my heart cried out for the fires to be kindled now, I heard the Lord say, "People who claim to follow me are spending more time fighting each other than fighting the enemy. This is delaying the harvest and blocking their destiny." I had been reading from the book of Judges earlier about the time when Jephthah was judge in Israel. The tribes were more willing to fight each other than join together to fight the enemy. They were causing more casualties among themselves than with the enemy. Friends, this should not be.

As these pictures and thoughts went through my mind, the Holy Spirit guided my thoughts to Psalm 19:14, "*Let the words of my mouth and the meditation of my heart be acceptable in Your sight, O LORD, my strength and my Redeemer.*" The Holy Spirit guided me through a few moments of processing these words. How often are the words of our mouths acceptable to the Lord? How many times have our mouths spoken criticism toward other believers and served to discredit them and their ministries? How often have the words out of our mouths actually been rebellion against God?

As I meditated on this and repented from every past word spoken casually, the Holy Spirit pointed to the second part of this verse from Psalm 19, "*the meditation of my heart.*" Control over the tongue must begin in the heart. The mouth speaks what is in the heart. Remember the words of Jesus in Luke 6:45, "*A good man out of the good treasure of his heart brings forth good; and an evil man out of the evil treasure of his heart brings forth evil. For out of the abundance of the heart his*

160

mouth speaks." We need to spend some time looking at the treasure in our hearts, because whatever is stored up there will eventually come out of our mouths. Will those words pouring out of our mouths be acceptable to the Lord? We need to really work on this because it is delaying the harvest and blocking our destinies. Can anything be worth that cost?

If unforgiveness or resentment is coming out of our mouths, we must confess, repent, and choose forgiveness. If jealousy and envy are coming out of our mouths then we know that these are the things we have stored in our hearts. We need to clean out the living rooms of our hearts and begin to store up the rich treasure of God's Word. Then when our mouths open we will be confessing Jesus and the power of God. Then we will be making decrees against the enemy rather than against other believers. Now is the time to be united in the Holy Spirit, fully armed for battle, and taking enemy territory every day.

Now is the time of the harvest! May we all be fully equipped to let our mouths speak the Word of God which is so richly stored in our hearts! May we let the Sword of the Lord come forth from our mouths to bring down enemy strongholds! May prophetic words be flowing from our mouths to buildup, encourage, and comfort the saints! Psalm 19:14, "*Let the words of my mouth and the meditation of my heart be acceptable in Your sight, O LORD, my strength and my Redeemer.*" Amen! Amen?

DAY 55

PRAY MORE WITH LESS WORDS

This morning as I asked the Holy Spirit to tell me what heaven is saying today, I cried out to know what would please the Father today and what would honor the Lord Jesus today. I immediately heard the Lord say, "Pray more!" My first thought was that I was asking too soon in my morning visitation with the Lord. So, I began to pray in the spirit. The Lord allowed me to go on for a while, and then said, "Pray more and use fewer words!" It was then that I realized this was the message from heaven today.

The Lord took me into a vision in which I saw many people standing around in various places and doing nothing. I saw a man standing in line at a government office doing nothing. I saw a woman sitting in a chair watching something on TV, and she was doing nothing. I saw other men and women doing nothing. Then I heard the Lord say, "Don't tell me you don't have time to pray! Pray more and don't use words!" For most of us this sounds contradictory. How can you pray without using words? We have been taught many prayer techniques and they all have something in common – we are speaking things to the Lord. So, how do we pray with fewer words or no words at all?

I was suddenly caught up in a different place without any awareness of the room where my body was still face down on the floor. I was completely caught up in a heavenly place. I was in a large open meadow where lush green grass like a soft shag carpet was completely encircled by a beautiful forest. Everything was green and alive. My heart was so full of joy and peace that I began to dance around the meadow as I experienced a deep spiritual awareness of being completely enveloped in the presence of the Lord. I knew what He was thinking and saying about me (without words). I knew that He knew what I was thinking and saying about Him (without words).

I was suddenly startled, thinking that I had drifted off to sleep because I was so completely caught up in this heavenly place without any awareness of where my body was physically located. This startling experience brought me back to the room which was disappointing, but necessary. Then I heard the Lord say, "See, that's how it's done!" The Lord had just given me a Psalm 4:4 experience, *"Meditate within your heart on your bed, and be still."* I was reminded again of Psalm 46:10, *"Be still, and know that I am God;"* Then, I heard the Lord again say, "Pray more and use fewer words!" Zephaniah 1:7, *"Be silent in the presence of the Lord GOD; for the day of the LORD is at hand, for the LORD has prepared a sacrifice; He has invited His guests."*

Obviously, there is a time to speak and a time to keep silent. Ecclesiastes 3:7, *"A time to tear, and a time to sew; a time to keep silence, and a time to speak;"* The gift is to know which is appropriate at any given moment. I believe we find it much more difficult to know when to be silent. I pray that the Holy Spirit will increase the gift of discernment so that we may know when to be still and silent before the Lord. I pray also that the gift of discerning the will and thoughts of the Lord will increase to the point that we are free to ask fewer questions. I pray that we may have more and more experiences in His presence when His love is so strong that all we need to do is receive it and soak in it with grateful hearts. Amen!

DAY 56

DWELLING WITH HIM

This morning, I was reflecting on the Feast of Tabernacles we celebrated during the past week. I was meditating on God's plan to dwell with us during the thousand year reign of Christ and in the new heaven and new earth. What an awesome thought! We are called to use this appointed time of the Lord to rehearse for the full manifestation of these promises in the near future. I was thinking about the rehearsal (convocation) we had been through. I reflected on the fact that we are rehearsing a future event while experiencing it now as Christ dwells in us and we dwell in Him and together we dwell in the Father. God has given us such a rich foretaste of a future and more complete experience. Father God is so amazing and so wonderful! Hallelujah!

In the midst of this reflection, I went into a vision. I saw what appeared to be a giant wing-tipped black shoe. I couldn't tell if it was that large or if I was being given a very close up view. The shoe was in the process of being shined by a professional shoe shine expert, and it now looked new! At this moment I began to see where the shoe had been. It had walked through very dirty places and the filth of those places of the flesh had attached to the shoe and had soaked into the inner most parts. This shoe had carried its owner into all the vile places of the earth and had been tainted by all the sin and corruption of the world. But now the master of restoration had made it like new again. Praise the Lord!

I thought that the owner of this shoe would now know better than to allow this to happen again. After being found by the master of restoration, he would surely be committed to remaining in that wonderful state of newness. But, to my surprise, the owner was sent out to go through the same areas of the flesh again. But, something was different this time. As the shoe walked through all the filth of the flesh it was not soiled or corrupted. Instead, every area where the shoe made contact in those dark places, they became clean. The shoe had been restored in order to recreate it back to God's purpose. It had been made an instrument of restoration.

Then the Lord said that as we have experienced His presence (restoring us) during the season of Tabernacles, we must now go out into the world as carriers of the kingdom of God. Standing in faith (in those restored shoes) we are to establish the kingdom of God wherever we touch the soiled surface of the earth. We are not to enter a place of rest, protection, and perfection until all has been fulfilled. Now is the time to be the instruments of restoration. I heard him saying we can do it because, "Now, I am dwelling in you and you in me!" The Lord reminded me of two passages in Leviticus:

Leviticus 14:14, *"The priest shall take some of the blood of the trespass offering, and the priest shall put it on the tip of the right ear of him who is to be cleansed, on the thumb of his right hand, and on the big toe of his right foot."* The right foot was cleansed by the blood of the offering from all the filth it picked up while walking in the flesh. Then, it was anointed with oil for the purpose of walking in the way of the Lord (cleansed and restored): Leviticus 14:17, *"And of the rest of the oil in his hand, the priest shall put some on the tip of the right ear of him who is to be cleansed, on the thumb of his right hand, and on the big toe of his right foot, on the blood of the trespass offering."* He puts the oil of anointing right on top of the blood.

God desires to anoint our walk and to transform us into instruments of reconciliation. I pray for an anointing to come on you today! I pray for an anointing of restoration and equipping for kingdom building! I pray that God will fully equip you for every good work as He restores you to the fullness of His purposes and your eternal destiny in Him! Amen!

_____

DAY 57

KNOWING TIMES AND SEASONS

As I prayed this morning, the Lord gave me a series of visions. In the first vision, I saw an arm holding out a new watch for others to see. The face of the watch was very large and displayed a beautiful classical painting. As you looked at the watch, the painting caught your attention rather than the watch hands. In fact, it was difficult to see the hands of the watch as they blended in with the painting. I heard the Lord say, "My people are buying more and more expensive and elaborate watches, but are less and less aware of the time. They are so focused on the beauty of the watch that they do not know the times or the seasons. Matthew 16:1-3, *"Then the Pharisees and Sadducees came, and testing Him asked that He would show them a sign from heaven. He answered and said to them, "When it is evening you say, 'It will be fair weather, for the sky is red'; and in the morning, 'It will be foul weather today, for the sky is red and threatening.' Hypocrites! You know how to discern the face of the sky, but you cannot discern the signs of the times."*

Next, I saw a young woman practicing on a very large keyboard. A metronome was sitting on the left side of the keyboard, and as I watched, the young lady turned it off because the sound was distracting her. I heard the Lord say, "Is it any wonder that your timing is off? You prefer your own tempo to mine." Daniel 2:21, *"And He changes the times and the seasons; He removes kings and raises up kings; He gives wisdom to the wise and knowledge to those who have understanding."*

Then I saw a small child sitting on a mother's lap with an adult watch on her hand. She was having fun with the watch as

167

she played with it and used it to catch the attention of others. An adult watch on a tiny arm is just a toy. The child had no idea how to use the watch to understand the time. She was simply using it to draw more and more people to her. Then I heard the Lord say, "Much of the teaching of the church concerning the times is used to attract more people, but like the child, the church has no real idea of what time it is in the kingdom of Heaven."

> *"But concerning the times and the seasons, brethren, you have no need that I should write to you. For you yourselves know perfectly that the day of the Lord so comes as a thief in the night. For when they say, "Peace and safety!" then sudden destruction comes upon them, as labor pains upon a pregnant woman. And they shall not escape. But you, brethren, are not in darkness, so that this Day should over- take you as a thief. You are all sons of light and sons of the day. We are not of the night nor of darkness. Therefore let us not sleep, as others do, but let us watch and be sober."*
> (1 Thessalonians 5:1-6)

May your attention always be upon the Lord and His times and seasons! May the wisdom of the Holy Spirit guide you to a full understanding as sons of light and sons of the day! May you be given a greater measure of the gift of discernment as you follow the leadership of the Holy Spirit! May all you do and say be pleasing unto the Lord! Amen!

WHO WILL YOU TRUST?

Today, we are departing on our visitation and ministry trip to Korea. We have been praying that we will be faithful in saying what we hear the Father saying and doing what we see the Father doing. This morning, I received several things that were specific to me and our travel. I then asked the Holy Spirit to tell me what heaven is saying today. Immediately, in my spirit, I looked heavenward and saw a huge head of cabbage. That was really unexpected. As I watched, the outer leaves were being stripped away and given to many different people. Even though many leaves were being removed and distributed, the size of the cabbage did not diminish. In fact it appeared to be growing larger.

I looked for an interpretation and the first thing that came to mind was the use of cabbage in American slang to mean money. So, I went to the Holy Spirit for help with the interpretation. The Spirit led me to Genesis 26:1, *"There was a famine in the land, besides the first famine that was in the days of Abraham. And Isaac went to Abimelech king of the Philistines, in Gerar."* And Genesis 26:12-13, *"Then Isaac sowed in that land, and reaped in the same year a hundredfold; and the LORD blessed him. The man began to prosper, and continued prospering until he became very prosperous;"*

For many people in the world, the current economic crisis has been a time of famine. Some have reacted in fear and have eaten their seed instead of sowing it. A general lack of trust in God's provision has robbed many of the blessings He has in store for them. I remembered the words of Jesus in Matthew 8:13, *"Then Jesus said to the centurion, 'Go your way; and as you have believed, so let it be done for you.' And his servant was healed that same hour.*" The way many Christians believe would have left the servant without a healing. We have gone through a time which has tested our faith. A few months ago, the Lord asked me, "Are you going to trust me or the market?" The answer was easy. As for me and my household, we are going to trust the Lord.

I believe that the vision this morning is a call back to trust. Trust that the Lord will provide for your needs. Then go one step further. Believe that He will also continue to provide seed for you to sow. In order to truly prosper you must have both personal provision and seed. Isn't that what the Lord promises to you and to me? Isaiah 55:10-11 (NIV), "*As the rain and the snow come down from heaven, and do not return to it without watering the earth and making it bud and flourish, so that it yields seed for the sower and bread for the eater, so is my word that goes out from my mouth: It will not return to me empty, but will accomplish what I desire and achieve the purpose for which I sent it.*" The only promise given to the one who does not sow is "crop failure."

We are living in times that not only challenge our faith, but also give us the opportunity to let our faith grow as we experience God as the original promise keeper. Trust in the Lord and see what He will do. Malachi 3:10-11, "'*Bring all the tithes into the storehouse, that there may be food in My house, and try Me now in this,' Says the Lord of hosts, 'If I will not open for you the windows of heaven and pour out for you such blessing that there will not be room enough to receive it. And I will rebuke the devourer for your sakes, so that he will not destroy the fruit of your ground, nor shall the vine fail to bear fruit for you in the field,' says the Lord of hosts;*" I don't know about you, but I want the devourer to be rebuked so that he cannot steal, kill or destroy any more of my provision from the Lord.

May the Lord bless you with an abundance of faith! May this be a time for you to grow in your trust for the Lord! May you experience an open heaven with the provision of the Lord being poured out in such abundance that you cannot contain it! May you have more seed to sow in the kingdom! May you increase more and more in accordance with the promises of the Lord! Amen!

KEEPER OF LOST THINGS

I was lifted up to heaven in a vision. I was led into a room filled with what looked like antique furniture and all types of old memorabilia. It was a fascinating place to visit. All the furnishings and keepsakes were from a time before I lived on earth. I was then introduced to a very old man who seemed both frail and agile at the same time. I was told by the Holy Spirit that he was the keeper of lost things (things and not people).

He said that he had something for me as he walked slowly across the room. He bent over and opened a tiny round (column shaped) safe that was also being used as a lamp stand. He took a few items out of the safe, and asked if I recognized them. I vaguely remembered these forgotten items which had once been my great treasures, but were now without purpose or value. He asked me if I wanted to have them back. He extended his hand to offer them to me. I thanked him, but said that I had no need for them now. It seemed so inappropriate to think about possessing things in heaven. They have no useful purpose and weigh you down as they take your focus off of Him. I didn't want anything to take my focus away from the Lord!

I pondered this for a moment. How often have we let these little things take our focus off of Him and also off of each other? How many precious moments have been missed when we worried and grieved over tiny lost treasures which we will soon out grow? Going after the promised blessings of materialism has robbed us of the real treasures of life. The enemy has found so many ways to get into our lives through little material things.

This experience left me with a renewed value system. I don't want more stuff. I want Him! I want relationships and love which will last forever. 2 Corinthians 4:18b, *"For the things which are seen are temporary, but the things which are not seen are eternal."* How about you? What do you want? May you have an eternal focus which will guide you to make better choices for your treasures! I am so thankful for the Holy Spirit who is guiding you and me into more and more eternal truth! Amen!

DAY 60

PRAYERS BRINGING BREAKTHROUGH

Yesterday we spoke to a group of pastors and their wives in SokCho, Korea. This group has been gathering each week for a long time to pray for revival in their city? I had the opportunity to share with them some visions I have received about the coming revival in Korea and then give impartation for revival fire. This morning as I prayed, gave thanks, and lifted up praise for what the Holy Spirit released in the churches Sunday night and Monday morning, I went into a heavenly vision. I was above the clouds looking down on a great cloud of darkness covering the land. The Lord said that this was the heavy veil the enemy had placed over the people.

This was a second heaven cloud. But, as I watched a light burst through from below making a huge hole in the cloud. Light radiated upward through the cloud with great force. This surprised me because I had expected the light from above to penetrate the cloud. I asked for wisdom to understand this. The Lord told me that the prayers, praise, and worship of the people had the power to break through even the heaviest cloud of darkness. In fact that is exactly where the light broke through — where the cloud was the thickest.

I expected the Lord to send the light of His glory back through that opening in great power, but He said to wait. I didn't fully understand, but I obediently waited. As I watched, other holes began to appear in the cloud all over the earth. The cloud now had so many holes that it looked like a colander for washing vegetables. I thought that now was the time for the glory to break through, but the Lord said to continue to wait and pray until the time is right.

I thought that I would have to wait for another day to see the Lords response. So, I continued to pray for the coming revival. Suddenly, I was moved in the Spirit below the clouds where I saw something like shafts of platinum coming down and forming giant columns throughout the land. I thought it was strange for shafts of dense metal to come slamming down. The Holy Spirit gave me a closer look. These columns were actually made up of densely packed photons of light. The power of God's glory was coming down in greater strength than I had asked or imagined. It was awesome to see the power of His glory so dense that it appeared to actually be solid metal. He has so much more for us than we have ever imagined. May we give thanks to the God and Father of our Lord, Jesus Christ who blesses us with the power and strength of His glory! Amen!!!

The Lord said that we should not give up when the time for the manifestation of the answer to our prayers is so near. May you be inspired by the Holy Spirit to continue your intercessory prayers for a great revival as the great end time harvest is so near! May you be more filled with a strong resolve to never stop — never grow weary — never grow tired waiting upon the Lord! The manifestation of the fullness of His glory is so near! Amen!

DAY 61

UNDER AN OPEN HEAVEN

This morning in our worship time we rejoiced that the power of the Holy Spirit was so strong and the Love of God was poured out in abundance to us. As I was face down before Him, I heard the Lord say "Stir it up! Stir it up!" I immediately thought of 2 Timothy 1:6-7, *"Therefore I remind you to stir up the gift of God which is in you through the laying on of my hands. For God has not given us a spirit of fear, but of power and of love and of a sound mind."* The awesome power of God flowed forth as I repeated, "Stir it up! Stir it up!" As the anointing increased, I heard the Lord say "Fan it into a flame! Fan it into a flame!" Then I remembered that the NIV translated those same verses to read, *"For this reason I remind you to fan into flame the gift of God, which is in you through the laying on of my hands. For God did not give us a spirit of timidity, but a spirit of power, of love and of self–discipline."*

As I was spiritually stirring it up inside, I began to see portals open into heaven in many places around the world. I rejoiced that we are living under an open heaven and God is inviting us to receive in abundance and to visit often in the place where we are seated with Christ. I pressed in and moved through one of the open portals. I hope you will do that today as well. When I went through that portal, I was caught up in an awesome outpouring of God's glory. I was in a glory cloud of amber colors and fire. It was wonderful and I luxuriated in it for some time. I wanted to see more and was enabled to see the angels worshipping God in great glory. There was so much glory being released in heaven and that glory is the wonderful gift of God for today. Then I saw it pouring forth from the portals and being made available to everyone open to receive it today. I pray that you will receive the glory of God in abundance today.

I started to cry out, "Let it flow, Lord! Let it flow!" As I cried out to the Lord, I found myself in a beautiful pool of fresh clear water beneath a waterfall. God was pouring it out – the fresh, clean water of cleansing, refreshing, and renewing power of God. I was soaking it up and remembered Jesus' words in John 7:37-39, *"On the last day, that great day of the feast, Jesus stood and cried out, saying, "If anyone thirsts, let him come to Me and drink. He who believes in Me, as the Scripture has said, out of his heart will flow rivers of living water." But this He spoke concerning the Spirit, whom those believing in Him would receive; for the Holy Spirit was not yet given, because Jesus was not yet glorified."* I was joyously drinking it in. I wanted more and more.

As I received this fresh anointing of the presence of the Holy Spirit, my thoughts were on you. I prayed for you to receive this outpouring of the Holy Spirit in abundance. I prayed for you to receive the refreshing flow of God's precious spirit, today. I prayed that you might experience this refreshing, cleansing, and renewing flow today. May the Lord bless you and keep you in His love today and always! Remember to stir it up and then fan it into a flame! Amen!

DAY 62

A STORM IS COMING

This morning, I was given a vision from what seemed like a satellite view over the United States. I was shown a huge storm like a hurricane covering more than half of the USA. This massive storm was rotating in a clockwise direction and moving from the Northwest toward the East and Southeast. This is not the normal pattern for a hurricane. So, I knew this was about a spiritual reality. I heard the Lord saying, "A storm is coming! The winds of change are blowing!" Then I saw a large portal in heaven and something like the sun was shining down with radiant glory over the earth. John 1:14 (NIV), *"The Word became flesh and made his dwelling among us. We have seen his glory, the glory of the One and Only, who came from the Father, full of grace and truth."*

I didn't understand all of this so I asked the Holy Spirit to give me wisdom and revelation about the meaning of these two visions. The Holy Spirit helped me to understand that a change is coming which many people will see as a huge destructive storm. These people will cower and be immobilized by fear during this time. However, those who are led by the Holy Spirit will look up and see the heavens opened. They will hear the Lord saying, "Don't be afraid! Change must come! Don't be anxious! My radiant glory will shine over you and break through the storm clouds. My provision and protection will still be available to you!" I remembered John 1:16 (NIV), *"From the fullness of his grace we have all received one blessing after another."* Nothing on earth can stop the blessing flow of our God from the grace of our Lord Jesus. We will continue to receive one blessing after another.

As I looked up into that portal, I pressed in to go through it into heaven. As I moved through the opening, I was filled with such a blessed peace. It was so quiet, calm and pleasant in heaven. None of the storm or destructive force was present in heaven. I knew that the Lord was making provision for us to rise above any storm that comes. We just need to keep our eyes fixed on Jesus, continue to look to heaven, and receive by faith what God has provided for us in these stressful times.

Whatever storms may come into your life, remember God is unchanging. He has been with you through it all, and He will remain with you forever. I pray that God will give you the peace I experienced in heaven this morning. I pray that God will build up your faith to know that you know that Jesus is the same yesterday, today, and forever. I pray that God's glory will shine through every storm, and the warmth of His love will surround you, protect you, and give you blessing and favor, more and more! Amen!

DAY 63

NEW THINGS ARE COMING

Again this morning, I saw portals opening into heaven around the world. We are truly living under an open heaven and God is pouring out so much to us and for us. I pray that you are open to receive it and that you are standing in the flow of God's grace and provision today and always. As I gave thanks for this age of the open heaven, I began to see shoots of emerging vegetation springing up from the earth. Isaiah 11:1 (NIV), *"A shoot will come up from the stump of Jesse; from his roots a Branch will bear fruit."* I heard the Lord saying, "In the natural, you are in the fall season. The foliage on the trees is changing colors and leaves are falling as a sign of the approaching winter. But, in the spiritual realm, it is springtime, and I am bringing up the shoots of new things." I encourage you in this spiritual spring time to embrace the new things! Sing new songs! Let the Lord bring up fresh new things in your spirit! I recommend you do what I did and meditate on the two passages below:

> *"See, the former things have taken place, and new things I declare; before they spring into being I announce them to you."* (Isaiah 42:9, NIV)

> *"You have heard these things; look at them all. Will you not admit them? "From now on I will tell you of new things, of hidden things unknown to you. They are created now, and not long ago; you have not heard of them before today. So you cannot say, 'Yes, I knew of them.'"* (Isaiah 48:6-7, NIV)

After reflecting on this word, I noticed that the new shoots sprang forth in fullness. Leaves were coming up fully developed. Fruit was coming forth ripe for the harvest. This spoke to me of another great acceleration in the spiritual realm. We need to be ready to move quickly from a season of planting to the season of harvest. When the Lord begins to move, things will move very fast. Now is the time to prepare our hearts! Now is the time to get ready to move very quickly in preparation for the harvesters to be released from heaven. Remember the message in Revelation 21:5 (NIV), *"Then He who sat on the throne said, 'Behold, I make all things new.' And He said to me, 'Write, for these words are true and faithful.'"*

As a portal opened above me, I pressed into heaven and saw the glory of the Lord radiating in great power. Much of the area was filled with the smoke of His glory. As I beheld His glory and worshipped Him, I saw a vision of a new day dawning and the power of the sun was bathing the landscape with light and warmth. We need a fresh anointing every day to keep ourselves prepared for what the Lord is about to do. These things should not take us by surprise. The Lord has been telling us about it for centuries. Lamentations 3:22-23 (NIV), *"Because of the LORD's great love we are not consumed, for his compassions never fail. They are new every morning; great is your faithfulness."*

May you experience the greatness of His faithfulness fresh and new every morning! May you stand in the flow of His glory and be prepared for the new things He is releasing today and each Day! May you be filled with joy and expectancy, fully ready to move as He moves and to speak as He speaks! Amen!

DAY 64

LIGHTEN UP A LITTLE TODAY!

The presence of the Lord was very strong this morning, and it was flowing around me like a field of electricity. Sometimes it was coming down from above, and at other times, it was coming up from below. Then it was flowing up and down at the same time. I love the flow of God's presence. In the atmosphere of his weighty presence it is so natural to make a Third Heaven visit. So, this morning, I was taken up very quickly and found myself in a great open field with very low rolling hills covered with green grass like a plush carpet. There were clusters of beautiful flowers everywhere arrayed in colors beyond description. In the natural, you can only see seven primary colors. In Heaven you see with the spirit and the primary colors seem limitless. However, you cannot describe them to people who have not yet seen them.

As I viewed this scene, children appeared and were filled with joy as they played games in this wonderful atmosphere. I saw someone watching over them who looked like a young loving mother. She was busy doing her tasks, but also watching over the children as they played. There was a beautiful look of peace and joy on her face. There was no worry that any harm could come to the children and it was clear that there was a total absence of threat in this heavenly place.

As I looked back at the children playing, you and I became children and joined in their games with complete abandon. I was caught up in the realization that in heaven we can become children again for play time and young adults when it is time to worship or complete our tasks. This was a wonderful revelation, and I am so looking forward to the time when we can freely do this. As I watched the children playing, my heart was filling up with joy, energy, excitement, and refreshment. It was wonderful in heaven this morning.

Then I heard the Lord saying, "Don't strive so hard! Take some time to play! It is more important than you think! Remember I created you this way! So much of striving is about self and not about Me. So, lighten up and take some play time! You asked me what would please me today, and this is it. I am pleased when you are filled with joy and enjoying the life I have given you." Sometimes we forget that the Lord likes to play too. Then I heard the Lord saying, "When you play like this (free from worry and anxiety) it speaks of your faith in me to protect you. When you play like this (without shame or condemnation) it speaks of you confidence that I have redeemed you from all sin. When you play like this, you make a joy filled habitation for My Holy Spirit."

As we experienced being transformed into children, I remembered the words of the Lord Jesus in Matthew 18:2-4 (NIV), *"He called a little child and had him stand among them. And he said: "I tell you the truth, unless you change and become like little children, you will never enter the kingdom of heaven. Therefore, whoever humbles himself like this child is the greatest in the kingdom of heaven."* Wow! He really meant it both spiritually and literally. So, how about it? Are you ready to play? Remember, Jesus was anointed to remove the spirit of heaviness. Think about it as you read and meditate on the passage below!

Isaiah 61:1-3, *"The Spirit of the Lord GOD is upon Me, because the LORD has anointed Me to preach good tidings to the poor; He has sent Me to heal the brokenhearted, to proclaim liberty to the captives, and the opening of the prison to those who are bound; to proclaim the acceptable year of the LORD, and the day of vengeance of our God; to comfort all who mourn, to console those who mourn in Zion, to give them beauty for ashes, the oil of joy for mourning, the garment of praise for the spirit of heaviness; that they may be called trees of righteousness, the planting of the* LORD, *that He may be glorified."*

So, lighten up a little today! Receive the "oil of joy" and let it soak into the depth of your soul. Let Jesus replace that spirit of heaviness with a garment of praise. According to the word of the Lord in Isaiah, this is how we become a planting of the Lord so that we are called oaks of righteousness. And, the amazing thing is that "He may be glorified." When we walk around without joy and burdened down with heaviness, no unbeliever looks at us and gives glory to God for what He is doing in our lives. However, when we are filled with joy and the enjoyment of life, the Lord is glorified. So, have some fun today and give the glory to God. Amen?

DAY 65

A GROWING DECEPTION

T his morning, the Lord gave me a vision of an open heaven with the Shekinah glory pouring forth in majestic and royal colors. Then, suddenly, my view was veiled by clouds. In a short while, the open heaven reappeared. As I watched and focused on the opening, words scrolled quickly across the bottom portion of the opening like banners scroll across TV screens as you watch news programs. By the time I noticed and shifted my focus, it was gone. I couldn't read the words. So, I asked the Holy Spirit to reveal the meaning to me. If I needed that scrolling message, I wanted to see it again. However, nothing happened for a long time.

As I continued to cry out for the Holy Spirit to tell me what heaven is saying today, I received some guidance on the two books I am writing, but I didn't receive a clear understanding of what Heaven is saying today for this message. I continued to press in and ask for help in understanding this. Then I heard the Lord saying, "In these last days, you are going through a time of great deception, and the enemy is working hard to veil the truth from the saints. This week (Halloween) is a special time for deception. Many people who call themselves disciples are buying costumes for themselves and their children which represent demons and witches. Many of them are saying the words of the season which are the words of the devil. Many are speaking of death, curses, hexes, and fear. They are confessing the words of the enemy and empowering his ability to deceive. The deception is so great that people think this is harmless fun which has no meaning. However, there is great power in the words spoken by born again believers."

I remembered Mark 13:5 (NIV), "Jesus said to them: *"Watch out that no one deceives you."* How great is this deception? Jesus also said in Matthew 24:24-25 (NIV), *"For false Christs and false prophets will appear and perform great signs and miracles to deceive even the elect—if that were possible. See, I have told you ahead of time."* Is it possible for the elect to be deceived? If not, why did Jesus give such a strong warning? I remembered Romans 10:17, *"So then faith comes by hearing, and hearing by the word of God."* We know this is true because it is in God's Word. So what comes from hearing the words of the enemy being spoken by so many in these days? Before I go too far on the negative side of this, the real power was in the positive message of the Lord. He said, "If you are feeling distance in your spiritual life, press in and continue to seek my face. I am still pouring out My Shekinah glory. It is available to you. When it is difficult to receive it, you will treasure it more."

It is so easy to get caught up in the negative side of things, but it is always positive with God. 2 Corinthians 1:19-22 (NIV), *"For the Son of God, Jesus Christ, who was preached among you by me and Silas and Timothy, was not 'Yes' and 'No,' but in him it has always been 'Yes.' For no matter how many promises God has made, they are 'Yes' in Christ. And so through him the 'Amen' is spoken by us to the glory of God. Now it is God who makes both us and you stand firm in Christ. He anointed us, set his seal of ownership on us, and put his Spirit in our hearts as a deposit, guaranteeing what is to come."* Wow! Thank you Lord for that positive message and this awesome promise!

If you have experienced some difficult times recently, don't give up! The glory of God is still being poured out on you. If you have had difficulty hearing His voice lately, just press in! He is still talking. If you have been somewhat overwhelmed by the enemy's words being spoken around you, stop listening and press in to hear from the Lord. His answer is always "Yes" in Christ Jesus. He will never leave you or forsake you! You can count on Him today and forever. He will never change, and

He will never abandon you! Give thanks to God who blesses you with every spiritual blessing in Christ Jesus! Amen!

———————————

FAVOR! FAVOR! FAVOR!

As I went face down before the Lord this morning, I kept hearing Him say, "Favor! Favor! Favor!" That is good. I like the Lord's favor. Well, actually, I love the Lord's favor. As I continued to wait upon the Lord, He gave me some words for the books I am writing. So I asked the Holy Spirit to tell me what heaven is saying today for all of us. I asked the Father to tell me through the Holy Spirit what would please Him today. The Spirit urged me to turn over on my left side, and I turned over.

Then I heard the Lord say again, "Favor! Favor! Favor!" So, I waited for more. All this time, I was seeing in my spirit the glory of the Lord pouring out. Then I heard Him say, "With my favor you can do all things! With my favor you can do the impossible!" I began to reflect on God's favor, and I said, Lord, I really don't deserve your favor. The Lord said, "Exactly! That is why it is grace! It is my unmerited favor. It pleases me to give it to you!" That was great news, because I love to receive it from Him. 2 Corinthians 6:1-2 (NIV), *"As God's fellow workers we urge you not to receive God's grace in vain. For he says, "In the time of my favor I heard you, and in the day of salvation I helped you." I tell you, now is the time of God's favor, now is the day of salvation."* Then the Spirit urged me to turn over on my back, and I turned over on my back.

On my back, the Lord gave me a return trip to the home of the "Keeper of Lost Things." As I watched, the keeper retrieved a medium sized plastic box, removed the cover, and took out a very old diary. It was then that I realized that this was a vision of a time very far into the future. As he picked up the diary, dust tumbled out of it. The pages were so old that the edges had turned to dust and fell from the diary. Before I could be concerned about anything being lost, he opened the diary and all the necessary information was still safely stored. It was a diary of God's favor for our lives. We each have one. As he thumbed through the pages, I was reminded of how great God's favor is and that He has been giving it daily for such a very long time.

Then the spirit urged me to roll over on my right side. Then I heard the Lord say, "My favor was with you all through your past! My favor is with you now, and my favor will be with you forever!" Wow! All I could think to say was, "Amen! Thank you Lord! You are so good!" As I was hearing this, I knew it was a word for you as well. It is God's reminder that His favor is always with us and always will be.

May you take comfort and assurance from the Word of the Lord today! May you know in the depth of your heart that His favor is with you and that it always will be! May you know that the devil is a liar, and when he tries to tell you that you don't have God's favor, he is only doing what is natural for him! He is lying. Remember John 8:44c (NIV), *"When he lies, he speaks his native language, for he is a liar and the father of lies."* May you only listen to your Father in Heaven! He is truth and He always tells you the truth. Romans 3:4b, *"Indeed, let God be true but every man a liar."*

Remember what Jesus said about His ministry in Luke 4:16-19 (NIV), *"He went to Nazareth, where he had been brought up, and on the Sabbath day he went into the synagogue, as was his custom. And he stood up to read. The scroll of the prophet Isaiah was handed to him. Unrolling it, he found the place where it is written:"The Spirit of the Lord is on me, because he has anointed me to preach good news to the poor. He has sent me to proclaim freedom for the prisoners and recovery of sight for the blind, to release the oppressed, to proclaim the year of the Lord's favor."*

This is the year of the Lord's favor! This is the day of God's favor! "Now is the time of God's favor." Receive it! Rejoice in it! Give God praise and glory for it! Give God everlasting thanksgiving for His unmerited favor! Amen!

———————————

DAY 67

REMEMBERING THE SAINTS

As I prayed face down in my room this morning, I seemed to be surrounded by the dark clouds of the enemy which are bringing a great deception over so much of the body of Christ. In spite of what the enemy was trying to do, I continued to press in to the Lord's presence. Then I heard the Lord say, "There is a river of living water! Come, and drink freely!" When I heard that Word from the Lord, I really pressed in to get to that river. I remembered once more what Jesus said in John 4:10, *"Jesus answered and said to her, "If you knew the gift of God, and who it is who says to you, 'Give Me a drink,' you would have asked Him, and He would have given you living water."*

As I pressed in, I heard the Lord saying, "Come and drink living water to refresh your spirit, soul, and body. It will wash away all of the hurts, bitterness and un-forgiveness of the past and refresh you forever." I pressed in and could now see the river and the water, but I was not close enough to drink. I heard the Lord saying, "Come and drink the living water to renew your strength and prepare you for the breakthrough which is coming. Let it wash away everything left over from the enemy's work in in the past." I remembered John 4:13-14, *"Jesus answered and said to her, "Whoever drinks of this water will thirst again, but whoever drinks of the water that I shall give him will never thirst. But the water that I shall give him will become in him a fountain of water springing up into everlasting life."*

I pressed in again and finally arrived at the river. I knelt down by the shore and began to drink from the water. As I drank from the river of living water in heaven, I felt a great, wonderful, and refreshing flow beginning at the top of my head and moving down through my whole body. It was a truly awesome experience. I heard the Lord say, "Drink freely from the river and let it refresh, renew, strengthen, and empower you for your service in the Kingdom." I felt everything He declared, and it was very empowering.

During this visit to Heaven, I was thinking of you. I wanted you to hear the invitation of the Lord, "There is a river of living water! Come, and drink freely!" My prayer was and is for you to visit the Lord in the Third Heaven and be allowed to drink living water from the river that flows from the throne. Revelation 22:1-2, "*And he showed me a pure river of water of life, clear as crystal, proceeding from the throne of God and of the Lamb. In the middle of its street, and on either side of the river, was the tree of life, which bore twelve fruits, each tree yielding its fruit every month. The leaves of the tree were for the healing of the nations.*" Why would we ever consider going thirsty again when the Lord has prepared the refreshing, renewing, and empowering water of Heaven? Why not heed His voice, "There is a river of living water! Come, and drink freely!"

My prayer for you today is that you will be caught up into the heavenly realms and be allowed to drink from the living water! May the Lord open the heavens for you and lift you up today! May the Lord refresh, renew, and empower you to prepare for all the breakthroughs He has planned for you! Amen and Amen!

Remember God's plan for you recorded in Isaiah 55:1-3, "*Ho! Everyone who thirsts, come to the waters; and you who have no money, come, buy and eat. Yes, come, buy wine and milk without money and without price. Why do you spend money for what is not bread, and your wages for what does not satisfy? Listen carefully to Me, and eat what is good, and let your soul delight itself in abundance. Incline your ear, and come to Me. Hear, and your soul shall live; and I will make an everlasting covenant with you—the sure mercies of David."*

DAY 68

ONE HEAVENLY REALM

*"Praise be to the God and Father of our Lord
Jesus Christ, who has blessed us in the heavenly
realms with every spiritual blessing in Christ."*
(Ephesians 1:3, NIV)

This morning, I was given a visit to one of those heavenly
realms which Paul wrote about to the church in Ephesus.
I was caught up into a place filled with the glory of God. It
was as if the entire place was on fire and the brightness of it
made it difficult to see. At first I thought I was in a room, but
soon saw that it was much larger than a room. It began to look
like an expansive cavern, but soon I could see well enough to
understand that it was much larger than that. As my ability to
see increased, I could see trees and shrubs that were ablaze
with His glory yet were not being consumed. As I pondered
what I was being shown, I heard the Lord say, "This is the
realm of glory! It is a place of restoration in the power of God's
blazing glory. Here those who have lost hope can have their
hope restored. Here, those who have lost their sense of purpose
can have God's purpose restored in them. Here those who are
weary and wounded can be restored to health and vitality. Here,
those who need healing can receive it from the pure and holy
goodness of God."

*"And God raised us up with Christ and seated
us with him in the heavenly realms in Christ
Jesus, in order that in the coming ages he might
show the incomparable riches of his grace,*

expressed in his kindness to us in Christ Jesus."
(Ephesians 2:6-7, NIV)

I was then given a view from a greater distance. I saw people entering this realm of glory bent over with age, illness and difficult labor. I saw middle aged people who seemed to have lost their way entering the realm of His glory. I saw people who were sick and weighed down by the ravages of disease entering the realm of glory. I saw people who seemed to be weighted down by things which had oppressed and burdened them. I sensed that they had been betrayed and abandoned and were experiencing great pain from what they had experienced. My focus then shifted to those who were coming forth from the realm of His glory. They were all children laughing, playing, jumping, dancing, and running with joy and excitement. They had been so totally restored that even the effects of aging had been reversed. This gave me a beautiful picture of the goodness of God expressed in His desire to restore all things. Revelation 21:5, *"Then He who sat on the throne said, "Behold, I make all things new." And He said to me, "Write, for these words are true and faithful."*

I pray that you will experience the heavenly realm of glory and receive the restoration you need, today. I pray that God will pour it out from Heaven and bless you with "every spiritual blessing in Christ." I pray that whatever has burdened you, injured you, or weighed you down will be removed and all things will be restored by the goodness (glory) of our Loving Father God. Amen!

> *"He gives power to the weak, and to those who have no might He increases strength. Even the youths shall faint and be weary, and the young men shall utterly fall, but those who wait on the Lord shall renew their strength; they shall mount up with wings like eagles, they shall run*

and not be weary, they shall walk and not faint."
(Isaiah 40:29-31)

DAY 69

A SWORD IS COMING

As I was praying intercessory prayers this morning, the Lord suddenly gave me a vision of a very large sword which was several hundred feet in length. It was coming down from heaven and being thrust into the earth. Light was radiating from the sword because it was aglow with the glory of God. Immediately Revelation 1:16 came into my mind: *"In his right hand he held seven stars, and out of his mouth came a sharp double-edged sword. His face was like the sun shining in all its brilliance."*

I asked the Holy Spirit to give me wisdom to understand the meaning of the sword. As my eyes focused on the sword, I saw it being thrust into various nations, and kindling the fires of revival in the nations. I was led to Luke 12:49, *"I came to send fire on the earth, and how I wish it were already kindled!"* The first place the sword struck was Korea, and I prayed intercessory prayers for both North and South Korea. My heart longs for revival to break out in both nations and bring millions to Jesus. Then I saw the sword being thrust into the United States, and fires were breaking out. Next, the sword was thrust into Israel, and again fires were breaking out. Again, I was inspired to pray intercessory prayers for all the lost souls in the nations.

The Holy Spirit reminded me that the sword is also an instrument of judgment, and that it begins with the discerning of hearts. Hebrews 4:12-13, *"For the word of God is living and powerful, and sharper than any two-edged sword, piercing even to the division of soul and spirit, and of joints and marrow, and is a discerner of the thoughts and intents of the heart. And there is no creature hidden from His sight, but all things are naked* and open to the eyes of Him to whom we must give account." After the discernment phase, judgment comes to those who do not repent. So, I cried out to the Lord for all peoples to repent and return to the Lord who created them and who desires to be a Father to them.

Next the Holy Spirit reminded me that the sword is an instrument of warfare, and we are to take up this sword. Ephesians 6:17-18, *"And take the helmet of salvation, and the sword of the Spirit, which is the word of God; praying always with all prayer and supplication in the Spirit, being watchful to this end with all perseverance and supplication for all the saints. . ."* Our warfare is to be with words of knowledge and words of wisdom so that the Word of God can pierce the hearts of all the unredeemed. God and His angels will do the actual fighting with the devil and his wicked spirits. Isaiah 27:1, *"In that day, the LORD will punish with his sword, his fierce, great and powerful sword, Leviathan the gliding serpent, Leviathan the coiling serpent; he will slay the monster of the sea."* Our task is to take the spoils after the battle and return people to their savior Jesus Christ.

Finally, the Holy Spirit reminded me that the sword represents the imminent return of Jesus Christ to conquer Satan and his army, and then to rule and reign over the earth for a thousand years. Revelation 19:11-16 (NIV), *"I saw heaven standing open and there before me was a white horse, whose rider is called Faithful and True. With justice he judges and makes war. His eyes are like blazing fire, and on his head are many crowns. He has a name written on him that no one knows but he himself. He is dressed in a robe dipped in blood, and his name is the Word of God. The armies of heaven were following him, riding on white horses and dressed in fine linen, white and clean. Out of his mouth comes a sharp sword with which to strike down the nations. "He will rule them with an iron scepter."* He treads the winepress of the fury of the wrath of

God Almighty. On his robe and on his thigh he has this name written: KING OF KINGS AND LORD OF LORDS."

I pray that you will take up the sword of the Spirit today and let it purify your heart, renew your mind, and transform you soul! I pray that you will experience the fire of revival where you are located and begin to carry the fire into as many places as possible! The key to revival is for people to carry the fire out into the world where the market place, neighborhoods, and institutions are in desperate need of the Lord and the grace and peace He gives. May you be a fire carrier for the kingdom of God and kindle revival around the world! Amen!

DAY 70

NO FEAR OF MAN ALLOWED

This morning, I had a very unusual vision from the Lord. I was with a group of people in some sort of dark cavern. There was a lot of confusion on the part of the people about what we were supposed to be and what we should be doing. Suddenly, a very large hand appeared in the room with a piece of bread in it. The bread had a filling of very nutritious food. I took the bread from the hand, and was immediately subjected to heavy criticism from others in the room. Some said it was inappropriate to just reach out and take something from the hand. Others said I should have waited until I clearly heard that the bread was for me. The hand appeared again with another piece of bread. People just stood around looking at it and debating about what they should do. Some said that the time had passed when we could expect anything from the Lord's hand. Others said that it was some sort of test that we could only pass if we resisted the temptations of the flesh and embraced our impoverished conditions. As I watched, the arguing increased in intensity while the bread became stale in the hand of the Lord.

I prayed and asked for the Holy Spirit to help me understand this vision. I asked if it was coming from the Lord or from some other source, because it was difficult to understand. As I continued to pray for understanding, a stone was rolled away from the entrance to the cavern. I saw an awesome contrast between the darkness of our surroundings and a lush beautiful garden just outside the entrance. I was drawn to go out, but everyone else coward back away from the opening fearing that it was a deception or a trap. So, I prayed for guidance from the

Lord. Proverbs 29:25, *"The fear of man brings a snare, but whoever trusts in the Lord shall be safe."*

Then I heard the Lord say, "My people have been cowering away from the world for too long. It's time to take the bread of life into the world. All of this debating about what is correct and what is not correct has resulted in the paralysis of the Body. It's time to cast off the fear of those who press the politically correct agenda and do what I have told you to do. How can there be so much fear when you are in the majority? Cast off the fear of man and the anxiety about what is or is not socially acceptable, and stand on the truth of my Word. Now, go out into the world and make a difference!" Hosea 13:4 (NIV), *"But I am the Lord your God, who brought youout of Egypt. You shall acknowledge no God but me, no Savior except me."*

As I moved toward the opening, I was aware that not everyone was following. Many were still cowering in fear and confused by conflicting messages from the world outside. Then I heard the Lord saying, "If you are afraid to acknowledge me in front of them, how can I acknowledge you before my Father and all those in heaven?" I remembered His words recorded in Matthew 10:32-36 (NIV), *"Whoever acknowledges me before men, I will also acknowledge him before my Father in heaven. But whoever disowns me before men, I will disown him before my Father in heaven. Do not suppose that I have come to bring peace to the earth. I did not come to bring peace, but a sword. For I have come to turn a man against his father, a daughter against her mother, a daughter-in-law against her mother-in-law—a man's enemies will be the members of his own household."*

May we ask for and receive a Holy Spirit outpouring like the followers of Jesus experienced in Acts 4:29-31, *"Now, Lord, look on their threats, and grant to Your servants that with all boldness they may speak Your word, by stretching out Your hand to heal, and that signs and wonders may be done through the name of Your holy Servant Jesus." And when they had prayed, the place where they were assembled together was shaken; and they were all filled with the Holy Spirit, and they spoke the word of God with boldness.*" May we speak the word of God with boldness to bring light and life to a dark and dying world! Amen? May the Lord bless you with every spiritual blessing in Christ Jesus! Amen!

DAY 71

ARE YOU BATTLE READY?

This morning, I saw a great cast iron cooking pot with potatoes and vegetables cooking in the oil left behind from meat which had already been prepared. At first, it seemed as if a great banquet was being prepared, but I soon learned that these were battlefield rations prepared to feed a great army. As I prayed for understanding, the Holy Spirit carried me to a different area. Here I saw thousands upon thousands of soldiers mounted on horses lined up on each side and behind a great golden throne. They were ready and awaiting the orders to move out to the battle.

On the great golden throne I saw Yeshua ha Messiah waiting patiently for the Father's command to go forth and conquer. He was clothed in what appeared to be armor made of purest gold. I became aware that this great army was an angelic host. Each of them was fully armored in gold as well. They were giants compared to the people in the scene and their power was beyond anything we can imagine. Each sat on a horse of great size each of which was also completely covered with some sort of golden saddle, bridal, and war accessories. Each angel had a golden spear that appeared to be from twelve to fourteen feet in length. They were all completely still awaiting orders. This army was totally disciplined and made no move without the specific commands of the King of kings and Lord of lords who was their supreme commander.

I saw many people gathered in front of Yeshua and His great army. They were the redeemed who will return with Him when He conquers the enemy in the final battle of all time. This group seemed less disciplined although totally fixed on Him.

203

There was a great deal of movement among the people as they anxiously waited for the appointed time.

Then I heard the Lord say, "It is all a matter of the heart! Do you have the heart to go into battle with me?" I thought it should be obvious since they were there before this awesomely powerful heavenly host. But, then I realized that the question of the heart is always before God's people. Who do we have the heart to serve? During times of plenty, peace, and rest, we seem to have no trouble giving allegiance to Jesus. But, when the battle is near, we must test the heart again. Are we ready to do battle with Him? Do we have the heart for the fight? Do we have enough confidence, trust, and faith to put our lives at risk for Him?

This is a time to make choices. Where do you stand, and what are you willing to risk? Where is your faith and confidence when the battle begins? If we don't prepare our hearts now, we will not be ready when the time comes. I pray that we are all at the ready like this heavenly host standing beside and behind Yeshua. I pray that we have put on the full armor of God and sharpened our swords as our hearts are made ready for what lies ahead. I heard the Lord say again, "It is all a matter of the heart! Do you have the heart to go into battle with me, today?"

DAY 72

SEEKING HIS FACE

This morning, I saw an open portal into Heaven. I like to see these open portals into heaven. How about you? And when I see one, I press in to go through it into the realms of Heaven. As I watched and pressed in something different happened. I saw a portal within the portal. As I contemplated this, I saw a portal in the portal in the portal of heaven. I asked the Holy Spirit to help me understand. Then I heard the Lord say, "There are many realms in my heavenly places. The more you press in and seek my face the more you will open these additional portals." 1 Chronicles 16:10-11, *"Glory in his holy name; let the hearts of those who seek the Lord rejoice.Look to the Lord and his strength; seek his face always."*

I remembered the prayer of David in Psalm 27:7-8 (NIV) *"Hear my voice when I call, O Lord; be merciful to me and answer me. My heart says of you, "Seek his face!" Your face, Lord, I will seek."* I believe that it was this constant seeking the face of the Lord which resulted in God saying that David was a man after His own heart. This seeking after the Lord was taught to Solomon, and in his early days he too sought the Lord's face and received this promise: 2 Chronicles 7:14, *"if my people, who are called by my name, will humble themselves and pray and seek my face and turn from their wicked ways, then will I hear from heaven and will forgive their sin and will heal their land."*

A life committed to seeking the Lord's face results in open heaven experiences. Remember David's testimony in Psalm 24:3-6, *"Who may ascend into the hill of the Lord? Or who may stand in His holy place? He who has clean hands and a pure*

205

heart, who has not lifted up his soul to an idol, nor sworn deceitfully. He shall receive blessing from the Lord, and righteousness from the God of his salvation. This is Jacob, the generation of those who seek Him, who seek Your face." If you are longing to stand in "*His holy place,*" follow David's advice. Be as the generation of Jacob which above all seeks Him and seeks His face.

You are living every day under an open heaven and the Lord is waiting for you to press in to the heavenly places where you have already been seated. Ephesians 2:4-7, "*But God, who is rich in mercy, because of His great love with which He loved us, even when we were dead in trespasses, made us alive together with Christ (by grace you have been saved), and raised us up together, and made us sit together in the heavenly places in Christ Jesus, that in the ages to come He might show the exceeding riches of His grace in His kindness toward us in Christ Jesus.*" You have been made alive in Christ for this specific purpose: that you may be seated with Him in heavenly places right now. And in this age, which has already come that He might show you the "exceeding riches of His grace in His kindness" toward you in Christ Jesus.

This is not "pie in the sky in the bye and bye!" This is for the here and now in Christ Jesus. How tragic when people live under an open heaven and never look up to see it or press in to their rightful place in Heaven! Awaiting you is a portal in a portal in a portal into Heaven. Reach up! Press in! Receive what you need! And, then receive what the Lord has prepared for you.

I will close today with Paul's benediction from Ephesians 3:20-21, "*Now to him who is able to do immeasurably more than all we ask or imagine, according to his power that is at work within us, to him be glory in the church and in Christ Jesus throughout all generations, for ever and ever! Amen.*" Remember, He gives above and beyond what you have asked or imagined. May you receive all that God has planned and offered to you!

DAY 73

WINDOWS OF HEAVEN

As I closed my eyes in worship this morning, I was immediately given a vision of a very large window into Heaven. The glory of God was radiating in abundance from that window. I spent some time basking in the glow of the glory of God. I thought of the windows of Heaven God declared in Malachi 3:10, "'*Bring all the tithes into the storehouse, that there may be food in My house, and try Me now in this,' says the LORD of hosts, '"If I will not open for you the windows of heaven and pour out for you such blessing that there will not be room enough to receive it."'* I don't know about you, but I love for the windows of heaven to be open to me. Those of us who have sown much seed (the tithe and the offerings) should trust God's word and expectantly wait for the windows to open.

As I reflected on these things, I heard the Lord saying, "The world has placed a curse on Monday, and they are filled with dread and fear because of the things they have spoken into being." I thought of the words of Jeremiah, "*Death has climbed in through our windows and has entered our fortresses; it has cut off the children from the streets and the young men from the public squares.*" (Jeremiah 9:21, NIV) We know that "*Death and life are in the power of the tongue, and those who love it will eat its fruit.*" (Proverbs 18:21) Then I heard the Lord say, "It must not be like that with you who are in me! You should look into the Monday mornings in your life and see the windows of heaven open to you. You should see the pouring out of my glory, and celebrate Monday as the beginning of another week of blessing and favor. Remember how you are always saying, 'I am extremely blessed and highly favored!' Believe what you say and trust in my provision."

I looked again at the promise of open windows in Malachi 3. My eyes moved down to verse 11, "*And I will rebuke the devourer for your sakes, so that he will not destroy the fruit of your ground, nor shall the vine fail to bear fruit for you in the field,' says the Lord of hosts;*" What an awesome promise! Has the devourer been trying to destroy the fruit of your ground? Take heart! The Lord of host (armies of heaven) has declared that He will rebuke that devourer. The Lord of Hosts has declared that your vine will not fail to bear fruit. Hallelujah!

When it seems that the devourer is at the door, look at the open windows of heaven and laugh with God at the feeble attempts of the enemy to do you harm. Remember Psalm 37:12-15, "*The wicked plot against the righteous and gnash their teeth at them; but the Lord laughs at the wicked, for he knows their day is coming. The wicked draw the sword and bend the bow to bring down the poor and needy, to slay those whose ways are upright. But their swords will pierce their own hearts, and their bows will be broken.*" This is a good day to laugh with the Lord at the failed attempts of the enemy to rob you of your blessings.

May you see the windows of heaven open before you, and may you stand in the blessing flow of God's glory that is pouring forth from heaven today! Believe the Word of the Lord and laugh at the words of the enemy. Remember Romans 10:17, "*So then faith comes by hearing, and hearing by the word of God.*" So, read aloud the Word of the Lord today. If fear comes in or the flow of your blessings is blocked, don't start listening to the word of the enemy. Go back to God's word and believe wholeheartedly that the Lord of hosts has opened the windows of heaven over you and is pouring out more blessings than you have room to receive. In faith believe that you will have more than enough so that you can bless others with your overflow. Amen! Amen?

DAY 74

MOUNTAIN MOVING FAITH

This morning, I was given a vision of a man standing amid what appeared to be a giant redwood forest. But, these trees were much larger than any redwood trees on earth. The man was like an ant at the base of the trees. I said, "These trees are too large to be trees on earth." I heard the Lord say, "These are some of the trees in Heaven. I want you to understand that there are forces in the universe and in the heavens which are too great for human strength. You have no tools large enough or powerful enough to cut these trees down or turn them into lumber. Most of you have been depending on human strength and human wisdom to deal with the forces before you, but a season has come where you don't have the tools or resources to do it on your own. You are in a season when your main task is to increase your faith to the level of mountain moving faith." 1 John 5:4, *"For whatever is born of God overcomes the world. And this is the victory that has overcome the world—our faith."*

If we are to be "overcomers" and "world changers," we must build ourselves up in faith, NOW! Read aloud the instructions in Jude 1:20, *"But you, beloved, building yourselves up on your most holy faith, praying in the Holy Spirit,"* This is the season to be in the process of building ourselves up in our "most holy faith." Jude gives one powerful key. Spend more time praying in the Spirit.

We believe that God can heal and yet people fail to receive their healing. Why? Jesus gave the answer in Matthew 8:13, "Then Jesus said to the centurion, *"Go your way; and as you have believed, so let it be done for you."* Too often people are not healed because they have received what they truly believe

– nothing. We must add supernatural faith to our prayers to produce the results we seek. James 5:15, *"And the prayer of faith will save the sick, and the Lord will raise him up. And if he has committed sins, he will be forgiven."* The Lord is saying that now is the time to build up this faith so that when the time of testing comes, we are ready in our faith to deal with the challenges.

What kind of mountains are you facing? What are the challenges before you today that seem as large as those giant redwood trees in Heaven? Do you need physical healing or a miracle of financial breakthrough? Do you need healing in relationships which seem broken beyond repair? Are you struggling against the world's influence on your children? Do you need to take a faith stand among non-believers who seem to overwhelm you by their sheer numbers? Whatever you mountain may be, the answer is still the same. You must have faith.

The disciples were unable to cast out a demon and asked Jesus why. Jesus' answer is recorded in Matthew 17:20, *"So Jesus said to them, "Because of your unbelief; for assuredly, I say to you, if you have faith as a mustard seed, you will say to this mountain, 'Move from here to there,' and it will move; and nothing will be impossible for you."* And in Matthew 21:21-22, *"So Jesus answered and said to them, "Assuredly, I say to you, if you have faith and do not doubt, you will not only do what was done to the fig tree, but also if you say to this mountain, 'Be removed and be cast into the sea,' it will be done. And whatever things you ask in prayer, believing, you will receive."*

So, I am praying today for more faith for you and for me. I want us to have a mountain moving faith, and I am asking God to give it to us in the measure we need. Amen! One more reminder: Romans 10:17, *"So then faith comes by hearing, and hearing by the word of God."* Fill your spirit with the Word of God and the faith will come with it. Amen?

THE STAGE IS SET

This morning in worship I was carried in the Spirit to a very large auditorium (like Radio City Music Hall). The seating was in a semi-circle slopping down toward the front, with the back seats high above the front seats. There was also a very large balcony above. As I looked toward the stage, my eyes examined the huge stage curtains which were about 75 feet tall and a couple of hundred feet wide. They appeared to be of a very heavy fabric and were the color of purple. The stage had a very high gloss finish and reflected the light that was focused on it from the large spotlights above.

Several spotlights were focused toward the center of the stage and moving in circles overlapping each other as the lights in a theater which direct your attention to the area where the next performance will begin. The lights were of an emerald green and as they swept across the stage, it had the appearance of being a sea of emerald glass. I immediately thought of the throne room experience John report in Revelation 4:2-3, 6, "*Immediately I was in the Spirit; and behold, a throne set in heaven, and One sat on the throne. And He who sat there was like a jasper and a sardius stone in appearance; and there was a rainbow around the throne, in appearance like an emerald. . . .Before the throne there was a sea of glass, like crystal. And in the midst of the throne, and around the throne, were four living creatures full of eyes in front and in back.*"

All eyes were on that stage and the emerald colored lights that seemed to dance over it. Suddenly, the Lord appeared through the curtains like a blazing fire of amber color. Fire was going out from His presence in every direction and the power of God was flowing forth so that it took my breath away. Then I heard the Lord ask, "Why are you here? Did you come to be entertained? Or, did you come to hear my words and receive my commands? Did you come prepared to do what I say?"

No one spoke a word back to the Lord. There was a stunned silence in this vast assembly of God's people. How can we answer a question like that? He knows our hearts and we cannot escape His knowledge of the truth. I sensed that most of us would not admit it but we would like to see a show of signs and wonders. We would like to have an awesome story to tell the folks at home. But, it was clear that this was the wrong answer to the Lord's questions. So many people go to churches to be entertained and they are always on the lookout for a more entertaining, pastor, church, or worship team. But, how can you confess that to the Lord?

Are we really ready to hear what He says and go out into the world saying what we hear Him say? Are we really ready to see what He is doing and then go out and do the same things? That kind of lifestyle got Jesus crucified. The Lord's questions were and are challenging. How do we answer the Lord? You cannot get away with anything less than the whole truth. I knew that we needed to confess first and after repentance begin to follow His commands. But, in the vision, no one spoke a word. Everyone knew the answers to the questions, but had to make some serious decisions about their answers.

His words continue to work in my soul: "Why are you here? Did you come to be entertained? Or, did you come to hear my words and receive my commands? Did you come prepared to do what I say?" More than anything, I want to do what I see Him doing and say what I hear Him saying! At the same time, I know me and He knows me better that I will ever know myself. How do we answer the one who knows our every thought and impulse? May the Holy Spirit lead you today in giving the Lord your answers! Amen!

DAY 76

OVERCOMING BARRENNESS

This morning I saw in a vision a vast wasteland which looked like a desert wilderness. It had a certain beauty because of the shapes, colors and design, but it was basically useless. It was not bearing any fruit or providing any useful place for people to live and thrive under God's care. As I pondered this scene, I heard the Lord say, "This place became barren because of the sin of my people. It was once a thriving place filled with plants and trees bearing fruit and food for my people. But, when they no longer listened to me and began to attribute it to the god of this world, I withheld the rain. Look now at the results of persistent disobedience."

I was reminded of 2 Corinthians 4:4 (NIV), *"The god of this age has blinded the minds of unbelievers, so that they cannot see the light of the gospel of the glory of Christ, who is the image of God."* It is tragic when the minds of unbelievers are blinded by Satan. How much more tragic when God's people allow themselves to be blinded in the same way? Even Solomon in all his wisdom built temples for Chemosh and Molech after God had said that they were detestable to Him. Haven't we done the same things? In our nations, we sacrifice our children to abortion, affirm alternate lifestyles which God detests, we trust more in money than we trust in the Lord who gives true riches. We allow other gods to have an equal place in our nations with the one true creator God. A time of judgment is at hand for those nations which do not serve the one and only Living God.

The Lord then reminded me that there is still time for people to repent and return. 2 Chronicles 7:13-14, *"When I shut up heaven and there is no rain, or command the locusts to devour*

213

the land, or send pestilence among My people, if My people who are called by My name will humble themselves, and pray and seek My face, and turn from their wicked ways, then I will hear from heaven, and will forgive their sin and heal their land." In a time of economic crisis many have experienced the heavens being closed. But it is not to be that way for those who continue to love, worship and serve the God and Father of our Lord, Jesus Christ. We are to be under an open heaven.

Again, I felt a call of God for us to be in repentance for our nations and all the nations of the world. If we are called by His name, we heed His word, and humble ourselves in prayer as we seek His face. May we be in prayer that our nations will turn from their wicked ways and hear from heaven once again! May we cry out to our God to forgive our personal and corporate sin and to heal our land! May God fill our hearts with such a profound love for the lost that our prayers will flow naturally like a river of tears! Like Jeremiah, the weeping prophet, may we weep over the sins of our people as we pray for God to withhold His judgment and release more of the Spirit of grace upon us!

I was reminded again this morning that God is looking for those who are willing to intercede. Ezekiel 22:29-30, "*The people of the land have used oppressions, committed robbery, and mistreated the poor and needy; and they wrongfully oppress the stranger. So I sought for a man among them who would make a wall, and stand in the gap before Me on behalf of the land, that I should not destroy it; but I found no one.*"

Are you ready to build a wall of intercessory prayer and stand in the gap that the judgment of the Lord may be withheld? God is still seeking those who will call the nations to return to Him so that He can pour out the blessings of heaven upon them. Are you one of those individuals God is calling today?

(The Next Morning)

Yesterday, we were very busy and in the midst of several interruptions, I didn't get the final part of the message written down for you. After seeing this desolate plain and the consequences of sin, I was taken to Heaven and spent time in the garden. It was rich, fertile, and abundant with fruit. I saw the fruit of the month on the trees. They looked like huge grapes but the clusters were growing upside down on the trees. The Lord said that this was God's plan for us even while we are on the earth. It is His desire and plan for us to live in abundance even in times of famine. We need to pray as Jesus taught! *"Your kingdom come. Your will be done on earth as it is in heaven"* (Matthew 6:10). What is his will for you? The Lord wants you to live in His abundance now. Jesus said, *"For to everyone who has, more will be given, and he will have abundance;"* (Matthew 25:29a)

This morning, I returned to the garden and watched as the angels harvested the abundance of heaven and placed it into huge crates for delivery to us on the earth. There was so much abundance that it was beyond counting and all of it was for us. As I watched the harvest, I saw that more grew back after each fruit was harvested. It reminded me of Amos 9:13, *"'Behold, the days are coming,' says the Lord, 'When the plowman shall overtake the reaper, and the treader of grapes him who sows seed; The mountains shall drip with sweet wine, and all the hills shall flow with it.'"*

As we live in obedience to our God, He will pour out His blessings upon us. Psalm 67:6, *"Then the earth shall yield her increase; God, our own God, shall bless us."* That is God's will, plan and purpose for those who are in Christ Jesus. Psalm 115:12-15, *"The LORD has been mindful of us; He will bless us; He will bless the house of Israel; He will bless the house of Aaron.He will bless those who fear the LORD, both small and great. May the LORD give you increase more and more, you and your children. May you be blessed by the LORD, Who made heaven and earth.*" May you stand in the abundant flow of God's provision today! May you receive all you need and more to share! May you experience the fullness of the blessing today and forever more! Amen!!!

DAY 77

FORGET ABOUT IT!

This morning, I was shown a huge letter eight (8) in the sky. It was ablaze with the fire of God. It seemed as if the fire was moving around the eight in a constant flow which caused it to continue to be written. Then I saw some black letters appear in the sky. As I tried to focus on the writing in the sky it quickly faded away. I asked the Holy Spirit to help me understand. I heard the Lord saying, "This is a time of new beginnings (the number eight represents new beginnings). The past has been written and has faded from sight. Don't try to focus on the past! Let it go so you can move forward into my new beginnings."

Too many people are holding on to the past and need to let it go. Some are holding on to past failures and sins. They need to repent, accept forgiveness, and let it go. God forgets our forgiven sins. Stop reminding Him (and yourself) about them. Some people are holding on to old hurts and offenses. This will only produce bitterness, un-forgiveness, and resentment. Forgive everyone and let every offense fade into the past so that a root of bitterness will not grow in your spirit. Focusing on the past will block your ability to move with the Lord into the new beginnings He has for you.

As I continued to look at this vision in the sky, I saw above it, a giant opening into heaven. The opening had a large black "cloud like" object in the middle which was blocking the flow of God's glory and provision. I asked the Holy Spirit to teach me the meaning of this object blocking the flow. The Lord said, "People who hold on to the past cannot receive the full flow from an open heaven. The burdens of the past will block the flow for them. Let go of all your past baggage so that you

217

can receive all I have for you." I was reminded of Philippians 3:13-14, *"Brethren, I do not count myself to have apprehended; but one thing I do, forgetting those things which are behind and reaching forward to those things which are ahead, I press toward the goal for the prize of the upward call of God in Christ Jesus."*

All of this came to me after I prayed to know what would please the Father and bless the Son this morning. I asked the Holy Spirit what we could do to bless Him today. The message was clear! Embrace the new beginnings and let go of the old things that hinder you. You have carried them far too long. Let God set you free today! Your release will please the Father, the son, and the Holy Spirit.

Isaiah 43:19, *"Behold, I will do a new thing, now it shall spring forth; shall you not know it? I will even make a road in the wilderness and rivers in the desert."* God is ready to build a road through your wilderness and let rivers of living water flow through whatever desert you may be in. But you must let go of the former things to fully embrace the new things of the Lord. It is time to trade up from our pain, sickness, and sorrow. It is time to trade up to the full measure of the blessing of the Lord. I'm ready! How about you? May the Lord bless you with new beginnings every day, forever and ever! Amen!

DAY 78

THE WATCHERS

This morning as I looked up in the spirit, I saw eyes looking down on us. I heard the Lord saying, "I have sent watchers. You are not alone. I have sent watchers to watch over you." In a dream, Nebuchadnezzar saw one of the watchers who was bringing judgment on Him because of his pride. Daniel 4:13, *"I saw in the visions of my head while on my bed, and there was a watcher, a holy one, coming down from heaven."* Daniel interpreted the dream and said, *"This decision is by the decree of the watchers, and the sentence by the word of the holy ones, in order that the living may know that the Most High rules in the kingdom of men, gives it to whomever He will, and sets over it the lowest of men."'* (Daniel 4:17)

What I saw this morning was the watchers giving the kingdom of God to those whom the Lord has chosen. They have been sent to watch over the citizens of the kingdom of God on earth whether they are the highest or lowest. Jesus said, *"I tell you, among those born of women there is no one greater than John; yet the one who is least in the kingdom of God is greater than he."* (Luke 7:28, NIV) Whatever your position may be in the world, you are very important in the kingdom of God and He has sent watchers to watch over you for protection and provision.

Then the Lord gave me a vision as a caution. I saw people speaking critically of others. This seemed to displease the Lord greatly, and the watchers took note of it to report back to Him. We must be very careful to speak words of encouragement and avoid words of judgment in these last days. So many believers are burdened down by the word curses spoken by careless

219

people. These curses weigh them down and make it difficult for them to carry the message of the kingdom in power. Paul said, *"If you keep on biting and devouring each other, watch out or you will be destroyed by each other.* (Galatians 5:15, NIV) In 2 Timothy 4:2 (NIV), Paul gives this advice to Timothy *"Preach the Word; be prepared in season and out of season; correct, rebuke and encourage—with great patience and careful instruction."*

I saw the watchers watching over us, but also watching us to make sure that we are properly carrying out the commands of Jesus. Those who desire to receive the full blessing of the Lord must be about His business of encouraging, building up, and comforting their fellow believers. As the watchers are watching over you for your protection and provision, be assured that they are also watching over others for the same purpose.

May we so live and work that the Lord will be pleased! May we be a blessing to others: always prepared with a word of encouragement in season, and with prayers of intercession at all times! Amen! Remember 1 Thessalonians 5:11 (NIV), *"Therefore encourage one another and build each other up, just as in fact you are doing."*

DAY 79

BE OPEN TO THE FLOW!

In a vision, I looked up into a very dark sky above the earth which was also covered in great darkness. There was an open portal into heaven and light was spilling out and flowing toward the earth. The appearance of the light was like a cloud flowing as water from around all sides of the opening. The flow was gentle and slow moving. It was continuing to spill out, but it was as if the earth was unwilling to receive the flow of God's light. Great darkness continued over the earth.

I pressed in and moved through the opening into Heaven. The atmosphere seemed very different from other days as if preparations were being made for some major move. Then I saw a great white horse adorned with a gold harness and bridle. There was no rider on the horse, but it was standing ready to carry its rider into battle. Off to one side, I saw four other horses (off white, red, black, and pale green) with somewhat formless riders who appeared as black clouds. I immediately recognized the scene from Revelation chapter 6 as the seals were opened one by one. It seemed as if everything was standing ready for these end time events to unfold.

I was led past this area to an outdoor open amphitheater filled with people. There were long lines (about 4 abreast) waiting to get in. As I was led up an incline to be able to see into the theater, I noticed that it was already full, and I wondered how the rest of us would get in. I saw a stage area and all eyes were fixed on the stage. Somehow I knew that the King of kings and Lord of lords was about to appear to give the final briefing before the battle began. There was an air of great expectancy as this long-awaited event was about to begin. My thoughts went to the great crowd around and behind me who seemed to have arrived too late to get in for this very important time. I was glad that at least I was standing in a place where I could see the King when he appeared.

As we waited, an angel appeared and called some of us out of the line. We were told to follow him. As we followed, we were lead around to the side of the theater. There we were escorted to a row of seats waiting for us near the front. I had no idea why we were selected out of the crowd to be in these very excellent seats, but I was most thankful for this opportunity to see the Commander-in-Chief from this very good perspective. As I pondered this, I remembered the words of Jesus in Matthew 20:16, *"So the last will be first, and the first last. For many are called, but few chosen."* On another occasion, Jesus said to the disciples, *"And everyone who has left houses or brothers or sisters or father or mother or wife or children or lands, for My name's sake, shall receive a hundredfold, and inherit eternal life. But many who are first will be last, and the last first."* (Matthew 19:29-30) Though almost 2,000 years have passed, there are still seats for those who follow the Lord now – for those who are willing to give up everything to serve Him. If we are pressing in to be first, we may wind up last, because we are only seeking for ourselves. But, if we give it all up for Him and are willing to be last, there is room at the front.

All of these thoughts faded when the stage filled with light (not from spotlights, but from Him) as He moved to the center to begin His final briefing. His appearance was amazing! It was beyond description! I was so drawn to Him that I could see nothing else and think of nothing else. As I write this, I am reminded of the words in Hebrews 12:2-3 (NIV), *"Let us fix our eyes on Jesus, the author and perfecter of our faith, who for the joy set before him endured the cross, scorning its shame, and sat down at the right hand of the throne of God. Consider him who endured such opposition from sinful men, so that you will not grow weary and lose heart.*" In the end, He is the only thing that counts. So, don't wait until the end. Fix your eyes on Him now. He is not only the author of your faith, but also its perfecter. May we get our eyes off this world and the fleshly desires it brings and fix our eyes on the invisible world which will endure for eternity. 2 Corinthians 4:18 (NIV), *"So we fix our eyes not on what is seen, but on what is unseen. For what is seen is temporary, but what is unseen is eternal."* Amen!

DAY 80

A CLOUD FILLED THE TEMPLE

This morning, the Lord gave me two very different visions
for the day. The first vision was an assembly of people
who had gathered for worship. In this vision, I saw some people
who appeared to be Spirit filled who were stepping forward to
take leadership roles. However, the Holy Spirit warned: "There
are spies in your midst who are working for the enemy. The
spirits in them are counterfeit and not of God. This is a time
to be careful who you follow and always seek my wisdom
to determine if they are Holy Spirit led!" It is a time to be
cautious as the enemy is attempting to stop or hinder the next
move of God.

The second vision was in Heaven. The glory of the Lord
was like an ever expanding cloud. I knew that I was in the
temple in heaven, but I couldn't really see because the cloud
was getting thicker as it flowed toward me. I was reminded of
1 Kings 8:10-11 (NIV), *"When the priests withdrew from the
Holy Place, the cloud filled the temple of the LORD. And the
priests could not perform their service because of the cloud,
for the glory of the LORD filled his temple."* What the priests
experienced in the earthly temple, I was experiencing in the
heavenly temple. The presence of the Lord was awesome. I had
entered with the intent of ministering praise, thanksgiving, and
worship to the Lord, but I was unable to do anything because
of the thick cloud that now surrounded me. I stood in silent
expectancy unable to see how to move around or how to go out
of the temple.

Then, I heard the Lord say, "You are my temple, now!" I
remembered 1 Corinthians 3:16, *"Do you not know that you are*

the temple of God and that the Spirit of God dwells in you?" As I reflected on this word, the Lord continued, "I want to fill you so completely that there is no room for any other influence or presence of the enemy. I want to fill you so completely that it forces out everything else!" Wow! That is what I have been praying for you and for me.

The Lord was speaking of the fulfillment of the promise in 2 Corinthians 6:16-18, *"And what agreement has the temple of God with idols? For you are the temple of the living God. As God has said: 'I will dwell in them and walk among them. I will be their God, and they shall be My people.'"* The fulfillment of this promise began on the day of Pentecost and is continuing into these last days. It is time for us to begin to live in this fullness. It is time for us to allow the Lord to fill us to the point that nothing of the enemy can remain. That was not easy for me today. The enemy was working hard to be entrenched in my spirit, and it was a time of spiritual warfare. The weapons of our war are not carnal, but spiritual and mighty. I used the Word and stood on the promises of God revealed in the James 4:7, *"Therefore submit to God. Resist the devil and he will flee from you."*

God is faithful and will prepare our hearts to receive all of His promises. All we need to do today is follow the Lord's command in 2 Corinthians 6:17-18, *"Therefore 'Come out from among them and be separate,' says the Lord. 'Do not touch what is unclean, and I will receive you. I will be a Father to you, and you shall be My sons and daughters,' says the* Lord *Almighty."* In these last days, it is time for us to separate ourselves from our ties to the flesh and follow the Holy Spirit. It is time to truly be a temple where God can dwell, fill us to the full, and let His presence overflow into the lives of others.

May you be so filled with the presence of the Spirit that everything of the enemy is forced out! May you be so closely led by the Holy Spirit that you will accurately discern the spirits in others and never follow the enemy spies in our midst! May you be the temple of God and know Him intimately as Abba, Father from this time forward! May the presence of the Lord be more real to you today than the world around you! Amen!

DAY 81

HIS LOVE ENDURES FOREVER

This morning as I prayed for the Holy Spirit to tell me what heaven is saying today (what would please the Father today; what would bless the Son today; and what would bless the Holy Spirit today), I was lifted up to the Throne Room where I saw Father God giving messages to the seven Spirits to bring to us. The primary message from Heaven today is about the love of the Father for us.

I was given a vision of the peaks of several very high mountains. These peaks were of solid stone; covered with snow on the tops; and surrounded by clouds of the presence of the Lord. The Lord said, "These mountain peaks look very permanent and powerful from your perspective. However, they are temporary and fragile compared to the love I have for my people!" I remembered Psalm 136 in which the Lord tells us twenty six times that "His love endures forever." I thought "Twenty six times! Are we that slow and that dense?" Then I knew the answer. We are indeed that slow and that dense.

We only grasp a small portion of the immensity of the love of God. John spoke of how the Father has lavished His love on us. 1 John 3:1-3 (NIV), "*How great is the love the Father has lavished on us, that we should be called children of God! And that is what we are! The reason the world does not know us is that it did not know him. Dear friends, now we are children of God, and what we will be has not yet been made known. But we know that when he appears, we shall be like him, for we shall see him as he is. Everyone who has this hope in him purifies himself, just as he is pure.*" He has lavished so much love on us that we have been called "children of God," joint heirs with Jesus; and made one with the Father, the Son, and the Holy Spirit.

I was overwhelmed by the depth of God's love for us! We have only seen a small portion of that love. Back in the throne room of heaven, the Father was giving more words to the Holy Spirit for Him to share with us the depth of His love. In my spirit I knew that the problem was not with God's words or the Holy Spirit's teaching. The problem is with us. We have lived under the spirit of religion which teaches that we are worms who do not deserve the Father's love. We have been taught about a god who is out to get us, judge us, condemn us, and send us to hell if we don't say a little prayer. But, this is the god of this world being presented by the spirit of religion. The God and Father of the Lord Jesus Christ is doing everything possible to bring us to Him. Hell was created for Satan and his fallen angels. God is doing everything possible to prevent his children from choosing to go there with them. He doesn't want to scare us out of hell. He wants to love us into His eternal kingdom. He wants us to be in it now and live with Him forever. "His Love endures forever!"

I asked the Holy Spirit to do what Jesus promised: to guide me into all truth. This morning, the Holy Spirit made it clear that this is the truth: "His love endures forever!" I felt some of His frustration when people don't receive the positive side of God's truth; when people turn everything around and go back to judgment and condemnation. So, His message continues over and over: "His love endures forever!" When all those mountain peaks have worn down with time or have melted and been consumed by the fires of the final judgment, God's love will still endure. "His love endures forever!

May you feel the depth of the Father's love for you today! May you see more clearly that He is not looking for an opportunity to smite you! He is constantly looking for ways to tell you how much He loves you! He chooses to forget your sin so that you only see His love. He chose to send His Son to die in your place so that you could see the depth of His love. Choose the Father's love today! Give Him thanks and praise for loving you! Then you will please the Father, bless the Son, and bless His Holy Spirit! And that is what heaven is saying today. May we give abundant thanks to God for His enduring love! Amen?

———————————

DAY 82

A DAY OF REMEMBRANCE

This morning as I visited in the Throne Room, I asked what would please and bless the Father, the Son, and the Holy Spirit, today. I heard the Lord say, "Today is a day of remembrance. Spend time reflecting on what I have done for you; what I am doing for you right now; and what I have promised to do for you in the future. It is in the remembrance of these things that thanksgiving and praise will well up inside you and flow forth in worship." I remembered Jesus' words in Luke 22:19, *"And he took bread, gave thanks and broke it, and gave it to them, saying, "This is my body given for you; do this in remembrance of me."* By this command, Jesus instituted a time of remembrance so that we would not forget what He has done for us. Psalm 30:4, *"Sing praise to the LORD, you saints of His, and give thanks at the remembrance of His holy name."*

The Lord has also established ways of remembering what we have done. In Malachi 3:16 (NIV) we read, *"Then those who feared the LORD talked with each other, and the LORD listened and heard. A scroll of remembrance was written in his presence concerning those who feared the Lord and honored his name."* God has a "scroll of remembrance" for those who truly hold Him in awe and respect. We need to establish some method of remembering so that we will always be filled with thanksgiving and praise. These two (thanksgiving and praise) are essential if we want to be in His presence. Psalm 100:4-5, *"Enter into His gates with thanksgiving, and into His courts with praise. Be thankful to Him, and bless His name. For the Lord is good; His mercy is everlasting, and His truth endures to all generations."*

I was carried in the Spirit to a very large room that looked like a warehouse. It was several hundred feet long and about 200 feet across. There were some boxes stacked on one side which looked small compared to the available space. I saw some bales which looked like fabric or hay on the far left side of the building as well as a few scattered items in the remainder of the building. I was curious to know what this place was intended to be, since it is in Heaven. The Lord said, "This is a space to store up your thanksgiving and praise. No act of worship is ever lost or forgotten. Every offering is stored up for your future. This is a time to be storing up this kind of treasure in heaven." It was obvious from the vast vacancy in the room that we have a lot more that needs to be stored here.

The tie between these two messages became clear. To store up thanksgiving and praise, we need the remembrance to keep it flowing and to give it real meaning. We need to spend time regularly thinking of all the things God has done for us. We see that the Word of God is filled with these actions in Moses' books of remembrance, the prayers in the Temple, the many Psalms which recount God's mighty deeds in helping Israel, Stephen's recitation of God's history with Israel in the Acts of the Apostles, in the writings of Peter, John, Paul, Matthew, and others. God prepared a book of remembrance to help us get started and now we need to add to it what He has done for us, what He is doing for us right now, and what He has promised to do for us in the future. As we recite God's mighty acts on our behalf, we too are filled with thanksgiving and praise.

How will you establish a method or procedure to begin storing up genuine treasures of praise and worship in heaven? How will you find a way to regularly and consistently remember what God has done for you? Never forget that God is also preparing a scroll of remembrance and storing up our reserve of treasure in heaven. May the Lord bless you with every spiritual blessing as you open up the heavens with your thanksgiving, praise, and worship! Amen! Psalm 97:12, *"Rejoice in the LORD, you righteous, and give thanks at the remembrance of His holy name."*

DAY 83

THE KING IS COMING

During a time of praise and worship in Jerusalem, I was taken to the heavenly Temple and stood before the Ark of the Covenant. It was shimmering with the golden glory and the gold ornamentation looked as if it was on fire. It was a glorious and awesome sight. Priestly royal garments were laid out near the Ark in preparation for a heavenly worship service. The garments were crimson in color heavily decorated with gold threads in beautiful patterns over the entire front of the robes.

My attention was drawn to a very long line of priest with long silver trumpets raised up ready to be sounded. It was reminiscent of movie scenes in which the arrival of the king is being announced. 2 Chronicles 23:13a, *"When she looked, there was the king standing by his pillar at the entrance; and the leaders and the trumpeters were by the king. All the people of the land were rejoicing and blowing trumpets, also the singers with musical instruments, and those who led the praise."* There was a strong air of excited expectancy everywhere in heaven. Everyone was ready to fulfill the command of Psalm 98:6, *"With trumpets and the sound of a horn, shout joyfully before the Lord, the King!"*

From this joyful gathering, I was taken to the barren hills of Judea. The mountains had started to shake and everything was trembling at the coming of the king. Psalm 97:5, *"The mountains melt like wax at the presence of the Lord, at the presence of the Lord of the whole earth."* Again I was transported to a different location. I was standing on the Mount of Olives with a group of highly expectant watchers. I knew that at any moment the mountain would split, the Eastern Gate would be blasted open by the fire of God, and we would join the procession of the King of kings into the Holy City at His second and final coming as Messiah and King. (Acts 1) Hallelujah!!! Are you ready for it? Start now to prepare your heart for the arrival of the King of kings and the Lord of lords! There is no time to waste! He is coming soon! Even so, come quickly Lord Jesus! Amen and Amen!!!!

DAY 84

THANKSGIVING

It is Thanksgiving Day and we are so thankful to be in Israel to lift up our praise and thanksgiving to the Lord! This morning, the Lord said, "Every good and perfect gift comes from above — from Me!" I began to think of all the things God has done for me, but my human limitations in this world kept me from recalling all of them. However, only a small percentage of the total is an awesome collection of memories which causes thanksgiving to well up in me. Again, I heard the Lord saying, "Every good gift is from me and you should see the goodness in more of them." How often do we receive God's best and only see the challenge of climbing the hill. We need to keep our eyes on the prize-- the author and finisher of our faith. Thanksgiving welled up in me again.

Then I thought about our trip to the Temple Mount this morning, and how we entered His gates with thanksgiving. We then entered His courts with praise and thanksgiving. And, we were there on Thanksgiving Day! How awesome is that? I pray that today our thanksgiving will open the temple gates in Heaven and allow us to enter His Courts with praise! Amen! I want to share the testimony with you again. This morning we went to the Temple Mount and entered His gates with thanksgiving on Thanksgiving Day. We literally stood in His courts giving Him praise and thanksgiving. We stood in the place where the Holy of Holies probably once stood. Wow! What an awesome experience!

Later, we were back at the Western Wall, and I went forward with my written prayers to pray and leave in the crevices of the wall. After praying and placing my prayers in the wall,

I remembered that Kevin Basconi had an angelic visitation on the previous visit. I remembered that we get what we expect (believe), and I had not focused on an expectation before. So, I prayed for an angelic visitation or to experience some kind of supernatural manifestation. After praying in the spirit for several minutes, I placed my hands on the wall and leaned my forehead against the wall. As I did this, the wall disappeared and I found myself walking down the streets of old Jerusalem in Jesus' day. Everything was crystal clear (ultra HD). As I walked along the streets, I became aware that a crowd was following. It was a violent and loud mob, and I suddenly received by revelation that they were taking Jesus to the cross. The crowd overtook me and passed ahead.

My heart was broken as I watched what they were doing to the precious Son of God. I felt every blow and pain pierced my heart as they spoke curses over Him. I was overwhelmed by what He had to endure and the knowledge that He did it for me! I also felt a deep pain in my heart from the knowledge that He had to do it because of my sin. As I experienced all these things, I was trying to keep up with the crowd, but I could not do it. By the time I arrive at the destination, Jesus was on the cross. I believe that He had already died at this point, because He was aglow with the glory of God.

I watched as they took Him down from the cross and went with them as they took Him to the tomb. The tomb was slightly different from the garden tomb you can visit in Jerusalem today. It looked new, and there was no plastered area on the side of the tomb entrance. They placed Jesus' body inside and rolled the stone across the opening. I didn't move. I stood there for a long time. It was dark around the tomb, and I felt the deep darkness of this moment deep in my spirit. I knelt to the ground and wept for a very long time. Suddenly, a great explosion of power was released inside the tomb, and it seemed as if a nuclear explosion had occurred. Light blasted forth in all directions, and Yeshua ha Messiach emerged glowing with the glory of God.

As soon as I witnessed His resurrection, I was returned to the Western Wall. I had completely lost consciousness that I was located here in my body. I had experienced myself being bodily in Jerusalem to witness the death and resurrection of Jesus. At this point, a great anointing began to pour down on me. I felt the power. It was so great that small pieces began to fall from the wall, and I felt them hitting me. The flow of spiritual power was so great that it transitioned into physical power which was now manifesting in the natural world. I stood in amazement as I experienced these things. I am still amazed at what Father God can do! How about you?

This was such an awesome answer to my prayers for a supernatural encounter. This was an amazing Thanksgiving Day! Now I have much more to be thankful for every day. I pray that you will also have amazing supernatural experiences with the Lord which will fill your heart with gratitude and spill out in joyous times of thanksgiving. May we continuously release our praise to give Him glory now and forever! Amen!

DAY 85

YOU CAN'T HAVE
IT BOTH WAYS!

We're back from Israel, and all I can say is "Wow! Awesome! God is so good – all the time!" We experienced so much impartation, anointing, visions, and revelations. If you haven't been, go! If you have been, go again!" And please pray for rain. There are critical water shortages in the entire nation.

Last night, I dreamed three times that the Lord was saying, "You can't have it both ways! You must choose whether you will serve the god of this world or Me!" This morning in worship as I was face down before the Lord, I heard Him say it again, "You can't have it both ways! You must choose whether you will serve the god of this world or Me!" I immediately saw again, by the Holy Spirit, something which we had been shown over and over in Israel – the symbol of the hand of Fatima, daughter of Mohammed. Israel tried to blend parts of two religions and many have accepted the hand of Fatima (open hand with extended fingers pointing down) as a good luck charm. We were actually given a silver charm (for a charm bracelet) with this symbol at the Hotel in Jerusalem by a Jewish company. We got rid of it. There is no compromise. We cannot serve two masters. Jesus said it in Matthew 6:24, *"No one can serve two masters; for either he will hate the one and love the other, or else he will be loyal to the one and despise the other. You cannot serve God and mammon."*

We must choose! The Holy Spirit reminded me of the words in Joshua 24:14-15, *"Now therefore, fear the LORD, serve Him in sincerity and in truth, and put away the gods which your fathers served on the other side of the River and in Egypt. Serve the LORD! And if it seems evil to you to serve the LORD, choose for yourselves this day whom you will serve, whether the gods which your fathers served that were on the other side of the River, or the gods of the Amorites, in whose land you dwell. But as for me and my house, we will serve the LORD."*

This message came during the Christmas season. In this season, we are faced with the choice again and again. Whom will we serve - the gods of this world or the creator God who sent Jesus to save us from sin? What are we most interested in receiving this year for Christmas? I want the same thing I seek everyday – more of Him – more of God – more of Jesus – more of the Holy Spirit. I am so hungry and so thirsty for more of Him. He was so powerfully present with us in Israel, and I realized once again that I want more. The more I come to the living water and drink, the thirstier I become. I don't want to lose that thirst even for a moment.

The god of this world wants to steal that from us. He wants to take it away by dangling the goodies of this world before us. Every day, we are blasted with images of things we should want from the world. I believe this is why God commanded that we should not make any graven images. They stick in our heads and are very difficult to remove. Only the Lord can remove the images of the world from our minds. We need to renew our minds daily. Romans 12:2, "*And do not be conformed to this world, but be transformed by the renewing of your mind, that you may prove what is that good and acceptable and perfect will of God.*"

I want more of Jesus! How about you? I pray that the enemy will not be able to tempt us by the gifts of this world. I pray that every attempt by the enemy to draw us away will result in us being drawn closer and closer to Jesus. May the Holy Spirit impart a real hunger and thirst in each of us which can only be satisfied by an intimate relationship with the Lord all day every day! Amen!

DAY 86

ANOTHER TIME OF SHAKING

This morning, the presence of the Lord was so strong in our worship room. I could feel the power and smell the fragrance of the Lord. As I asked the Holy Spirit to tell me what heaven is saying today (what would please the Father and bless the Son and the Holy Spirit), I began to shake violently and for a prolong time. When the shaking subsided, I saw an open heaven and I heard the Lord say, "You are in the midst of a time of shaking. I am shaking things off and I am shaking things in so that you will be ready for the new thing I am about to release."

> *"When it shall be thus in the midst of the land among the people, It shall be like the shaking of an olive tree, Like the gleaning of grapes when the vintage is done. They shall lift up their voice, they shall sing; for the majesty of the LORD They shall cry aloud from the sea. Therefore glorify the LORD in the dawning light, the name of the LORD God of Israel in the coastlands of the sea. From the ends of the earth we have heard songs: 'Glory to the righteous!'"* (Isaiah 24:13-16a)

God is about to raise up a mighty army, but there must be a shaking first. Ezekiel 37:7-10, *"So I prophesied as I was commanded: and as I prophesied, there was a noise, and behold a shaking, and the bones came together, bone to his bone. And when I beheld, lo, the sinews and the flesh came up upon them, and the skin covered them above: but there was no breath in them. Then said he unto me, Prophesy unto the wind, prophesy, son of man, and say to the wind, Thus saith the Lord GOD; Come from the four winds, O breath, and breathe upon these slain, that they may live. So I prophesied as he commanded me, and the breath came into them, and they lived, and stood up upon their feet, an exceeding great army."* The Lord is restoring life to that portion of the church which has not been moving in the Spirit or operating under the power of the Holy Spirit.

We all need to have a few things shaken off so that we are better able to receive what God wants to release into us for His ministry and purpose. We all need to have things shaken into us so that we may receive and release the gifts of the Spirit for an end time harvest. It is time to stand under an open heaven and receive all that God intends for us. Are you ready to move into your destiny? Are ready to let go of everything that hinders you? Are you ready to receive what God is releasing? Are you ready to focus on His purpose for your life and mission in the kingdom? Then prepare for a little shaking!

May God shake things up for you today and any day He desires to release more of His Spirit into you! May you willingly let go of everything that is blocking your progress in the kingdom! May you cry out for more of His Spirit and more of His gifts. As Paul said in 1 Corinthians 14:1, *"Pursue love, and desire spiritual gifts, but especially that you may prophesy."* May the Lord give you your heart's desires! May He bless you with more than you have ever asked or imagined!" Amen!!!

Prepare for a repositioning and an elevation from the Lord. I saw an open heaven and I heard the Lord say, "You are in the midst of a time of shaking. I am shaking things off and I am shaking things in so that you will be ready for the new thing I am about to release."

DECISIONS ARE BEING MADE

This morning as I cried out to the Lord to let the Holy Spirit tell me what heaven is saying today, I placed a claim on Ephesians 2:18, *"For through Him we both have access by one Spirit to the Father."* I also placed a claim on the promise in Ephesians 2:6 (NIV), *"And God raised us up with Christ and seated us with him in the heavenly realms in Christ Jesus"* Then I claimed the promise in Hebrews 4:16 (NIV), *"Let us therefore come boldly to the throne of grace, that we may obtain mercy and find grace to help in time of need."* After a few moments, I was taken in the spirit (by the Holy Spirit) to a heavenly place which I could not clearly see. At first, I thought I was being veiled by the enemy and prayed to be freed from the veil. However, it persisted. Then I understood. I was in the Throne Room, and it was filled with smoke. I could see vaguely through the smoke enough to know where I was, but not enough to see clearly what my heart desired to see — Him!

As I continued trying to clear my vision, I heard the Holy Spirit say, "The Father is in the Temple, and decisions are being made!" Occasionally fire would break through the smoke and I would hear those words from the Holy Spirit again: "The Father is in the Temple, and decisions are being made!" In my heart, I was thinking: "This can't be good!" So, I fell on my face in repentance and said three times, "Here I am! Use me!" I began to shake violently (especially in my mid-section) as a familiar chill of the supercharged presence of God came over me. I knew something was again being shaken out, but what was most clear was that something was being shaken in. I felt like I was receiving a supercharged impartation from the Lord.

I knew that I was being prepared for His purpose, and I am patiently waiting to see what that will be.

At the same time, I knew that this was not just for me. It was for you also. After all, I had already prayed for you – that the Lord would impart something to you today to prepare you for greater work in the kingdom. I knew that everything which was happening was for all of us. And, I am imparting this to you today! Be prepared in repentance! Make yourself available! Open up your heart to receive the impartation from the Lord! Willingly accept your kingdom assignment today.

Then, I heard the Holy Spirit saying, "How will you stand in the valley of decision?" These words from the Holy Spirit led me to Joel 3:14-18, "*Multitudes, multitudes in the valley of decision! For the day of the LORD is near in the valley of decision. The sun and moon will grow dark, and the stars will diminish their brightness. The LORD also will roar from Zion, and utter His voice from Jerusalem; the heavens and earth will shake; but the LORD will be a shelter for His people, and the strength of the children of Israel. "So you shall know that I am the LORD your God, dwelling in Zion My holy mountain. Then Jerusalem shall be holy, and no aliens shall ever pass through her again." And it will come to pass in that day that the mountains shall drip with new wine, the hills shall flow with milk, and all the brooks of Judah shall be flooded with water; a fountain shall flow from the house of the LORD and water the Valley of Acacias.*"

This question is also for you. "How will you stand in the valley of decision?" Are you preparing for the Day of the Lord? It is certainly drawing near, and each of us must be ready to stand in the valley of decision. The Lord is in His Holy Temple, and decisions are being made. His decisions will be heavily influenced by the decisions we make today and every day.

May the Lord bless you with a great impartation of His power, grace, love, and mercy today! May the Lord speak to your heart through the Holy Spirit, and may He guide you into all truth! Some of the truth hurts for a while, but if we respond to His chastisement, we are prepared for the Day of the Lord. Amen?

DAY 88

DESTINIES BEING RELEASED

T his morning Heaven was filled with thunder, lightning, rumbling, and smoke. There was much more light in the Throne Room this morning. I knew that something had shifted. Then I heard the Lord saying, "This has been a year of judgment. You are now entering a year of grace! Destinies have been established, but people must step into them!" My mind immediately went to the scripture I had prayed a few minutes before: 2 Chronicles 7:14, *"if My people who are called by My name will humble themselves, and pray and seek My face, and turn from their wicked ways, then I will hear from heaven, and will forgive their sin and heal their land."*

These are the closing days of the year of judgment, and the wise will use them wisely. These are the closing days when the Lord is calling us to humility, repentance, and prayer as we seek His face. These are days to hear from heaven, receive His forgiveness for our nations, and to receive the healing of our lands. Are you crying out to the Lord as I have been doing throughout this year? Are you seeking the healing of the land in God's way or have you accepted the way of the principalities, powers, and rulers of this dark world? We are truly in the valley of decision in these closing moments of the year of judgment. Are you ready to step into the destiny Father God has established for your life and ministry? As in the days of Joshua, we must take up the covenant and step into the water to release the power of God into our spirits for the warfare ahead.

Then I heard a promise from the Lord: Malachi 4:2a, *"But to you who fear My name the Sun of Righteousness shall arise with healing in His wings;"* I heard this verse a second time, but it was slightly different. I saw it spelled out: "the <u>Son</u> of Righteousness shall arise with healing in His wings." All the nations of the world stand in desperate need of healing. The Lord has repeatedly spoken and called on true intercessors to repent on behalf of their nations, seek His face, and receive the healing of the nations.

Then I heard the Lord say again, "This has been a year of judgment. You are now entering a year of grace! Destinies have been established, but people must step into them!" This time the Holy Spirit led me to Jeremiah 29:11-13, "*'For I know the plans I have for you,' declares the LORD, 'plans to prosper you and not to harm you, plans to give you hope and a future. Then you will call upon me and come and pray to me, and I will listen to you. You will seek me and find me when you seek me with all your heart.'*" Destinies have been established for all of God's people. Are you willing to receive your destiny and step out in faith to accomplish God's purpose in your life? We have been so thoroughly trained to establish ourselves in the systems of the world, to rise to the top, and to take what we deserve. The challenge is to lay all of these things aside, and take up the destiny Father God has established for us. It is a difficult choice to make as we stand today in the valley of decision. However, we must consider how we will answer when we stand before the judgment seat of Christ!

For those who choose wisely, the promises are so magnificent. Psalm 24:3-6, "*Who may ascend into the hill of the Lord? Or who may stand in His holy place? He who has clean hands and a pure heart, who has not lifted up his soul to an idol, nor sworn deceitfully. He shall receive blessing from the Lord, and righteousness from the God of his salvation. This is Jacob, the generation of those who seek Him, who seek Your face.*"

May you hear the voice of the Lord from heaven today! May you seek Him with all your heart and find Him! May you receive blessing from the Lord and righteousness from the God of your salvation! May you choose wisely which destiny you will follow! Amen!

INSPIRED TO PRAISE

This morning, during my Bible study time, the sweet fragrance of Jesus came into the room. I felt (through the fragrance) that He was leaning over my shoulder as I read the first chapter of Revelation. This happened several times. Each time, I had to stop reading and just celebrate and luxuriate in His sweet presence. I didn't know if I would ever finish that chapter, but it didn't really matter as long as He was present. Later, as I went up to worship, that presence (the Holy Spirit goose bumps) was all over me. I knew that something special was going to happen today. I pray that you will feel and smell the sweet fragrance of His presence, and that something special will happen for you today.

As I prayed for Father God to reveal to me through the Holy Spirit what heaven is saying today, I was carried in the Spirit to a beautiful field of flowers in heaven. It was an awesome experience. The flowers were in full bloom and even the trees around this vast garden were covered with blossoming flowers. I heard the Lord say, "It is springtime in heaven every day! Everything is new every morning!" I remembered the words of Lamentations 3:22-23, *"Through the Lord's mercies we are not consumed, because His compassions fail not. They are new every morning; great is Your faithfulness."* Now, I understood that His mercies and everything else are constantly being renewed so that they are new every morning. Praise the Lord!

As I watched and admired the beauty of this heavenly garden, I noticed that in the middle of the garden flowers had grown up over something (a rock or a tree) and seemed to be reaching upward. I moved closer and could see that the flowers were raised up in the shape of two hands lifted in praise to the Lord. I remembered the words of the song, "All creation Worships You!" As I celebrated this, I had that really hollow feeling because the one part of creation which often fails to praise God is His people. In my heart, I cried out, "Let us all worship the Lord! Let us all bless His holy name!" Like those beautiful flowers in heaven, lift up your hands and worship the King of kings and the Lord of lords! Amen? I went back to that reading in Lamentations and studied the verses on either side of 22-23.

Lamentations 3:21-26, *"This I recall to my mind, therefore I have hope. Through the Lord's mercies we are not consumed, because His compassions fail not. They are new every morning; Great is Your faithfulness. 'The Lord is my portion,' says my soul, 'Therefore I hope in Him!' The Lord is good to those who wait for Him, to the soul who seeks Him. It is good that one should hope and wait quietly for the salvation of the Lord."* As I meditated on these words, I found hope that one day all of God's people will give Him the praise and honor due to Him. I celebrated that the Lord is my portion – the Lord is good. So, I will wait on Him in the hope He has given.

I remembered Romans 14:11 (NIV), *"It is written: 'As surely as I live,' says the Lord, 'every knee will bow before me; every tongue will confess to God.'"* I also remembered Philippians 2:9-11 (NIV), *"Therefore God exalted him to the highest place and gave him the name that is above every name, that at the name of Jesus every knee should bow, in heaven and on earth and under the earth, and every tongue confess that Jesus Christ is Lord, to the glory of God the Father."* If one day in the future, everyone will bow and confess that Jesus is Lord, why not NOW? Why not today? Why not right now?

I started to pray the words of Psalm 103:1-5, (Modified to be in the first person) "Bless the LORD, O my soul; and all that is within me, *bless* His holy name! Bless the LORD, O my soul, and forget not all His benefits: Who forgives all *my* iniquities, Who heals all *my* diseases, Who redeems *my* life from destruction, Who crowns *me* with loving kindness and tender mercies, Who satisfies *my* mouth with good *things, so that my* youth is renewed like the eagle's." *Baruch ha Shem! (Blessed be the Name) Amen!*

DAY 90

GOD DOESN'T PLAY
SECOND VIOLIN

This morning, during my visit to heaven, I was shown a violin standing on end with two bows crossed over it. It was slowly moving toward me. I said, "No one plays a violin with two bows. What does this mean?" The Lord said, "When someone plays the violin under the anointing, they perceive that they are playing alone. However, under the anointing, I am playing the same violin with them, and the real 'heavenly sound' is coming from me. It is the same with everything anointed people do. They perceive that they are doing the work for me. However, when they are getting 'heavenly results' I am doing the work through them." The Lord reminded me of Proverbs 3:6, "*In all your ways acknowledge Him, and He shall direct your paths.*"

If we acknowledge Him, He will direct our work, worship, and service. I wondered how many times, I have failed to acknowledge Him? How many times have I taken credit for what he actually did? It is humbling to look back at all our so called successes and realize that they were all His work. At the same time, it is exciting to think of the possibilities for the future if we will acknowledge Him and let Him work through us with our full support. As I meditated on this, I heard the Lord say, "Many successes have been decreed in the coming year! Will you acknowledge me and give Me the glory? My quick answer was, "Yes! Absolutely!" After considering my human tendencies, I added, "With your help Lord, I will acknowledge you in all my ways!"

My thoughts went back to Proverbs 3 and I reflected on verse 5: "*Trust in the LORD with all your heart, and lean not on your own understanding;"* This thought must always precede the action and acknowledgement. I believe this is the key for us in the coming season of the Lord. If you are going to move into the destinies God has established for you and have the successes He has decreed, you must — *"Trust in the LORD with all your heart, and lean not on your own understanding;"*

This teaching in Proverbs was so rich that I went back to verses 7-10. *"Do not be wise in your own eyes; fear the LORD and depart from evil. It will be health to your flesh, and strength to your bones. Honor the LORD with your possessions, and with the firstfruits of all your increase; So your barns will be filled with plenty, and your vats will overflow with new wine."* I don't know about you, but I am ready to lay claim to these promises for this new season. I want to please the Father, the Son, and the Holy Spirit. And, I want to experience all that He has planned for me. How about you?

A major challenge for those who serve as musicians in an orchestra is to gracefully play the second violin. Most people want to be first in everything. Understand this: The Lord never plays second violin! God must be first in all things. This year, I don't want to make my own plans and then try to get the Lord to make them work after I fail. I want to start with His plans, His decrees, His paths, and His ways! I want to find out what He wants to do and where He wants to lead. Then, I want to be available to go where He says and do what He directs. That is my plan for the new season.

I pray that the Lord will bless you with wisdom and revelation to know His ways and to seek His face in all you do! May the Lord bless you with increase, health, strength, and abundance for resourcing His kingdom business! May the storehouse of Heaven be open for you so that you can receive more than enough and an abundance to share! Amen!

BE STRONG AND COURAGEOUS

This morning, in a vision, I saw something metallic and solid emerging from a cloudy landscape. As I watched the clouds roll back, I saw that this was the shield carried by a mighty warrior. Then I saw what appeared to be a mighty warrior standing alone on a great battlefield. Slowly, I became aware that he was not alone. He stood shoulder to shoulder with a vast army of warriors just like him. Everything about these soldiers was dark, cold, and wicked. In the early light of dawn as the clouds cleared, they stood as giants and monsters before our rag tag little band of believers. My first thought was, "How can we stand against forces like these? How can all of us take on even one of them?" I heard the Lord say, "Your battle is not against flesh and blood! But, you must be strong and courageous!"

I looked for help from the Word and remembered what God said to Joshua as he prepared to invade the land: Joshua 1:9, *"Have I not commanded you? Be strong and of good courage; do not be afraid, nor be dismayed, for the Lord your God is with you wherever you go."* This was the third time the Lord spoke these words to Joshua in this passage: *"Be strong and of good courage; do not be afraid,"* Courage is not being unafraid. Courage is rising above your fear and doing what God commands no matter what the odds appear to be from a worldly perspective. We must courageously stand on our faith that the Lord our God is with us wherever we go. I took courage from these words. How about you?

Looking back at this awful army horde before us, I reflected on the words of an eighty-five year old Caleb in Joshua

14:11-12, *"As yet I am as strong this day as on the day that Moses sent me; just as my strength was then, so now is my strength for war, both for going out and for coming in. Now therefore, give me this mountain of which the LORD spoke in that day; for you heard in that day how the Anakim were there, and that the cities were great and fortified. It may be that the LORD will be with me, and I shall be able to drive them out as the LORD said."* The scriptures simply say in Joshua 15:14, *"Caleb drove out the three sons of Anak from there: Sheshai, Ahiman, and Talmai, the children of Anak."* The giants did not frighten Caleb, because he trusted in the Lord and in the strength God gave him for war. This strength from the Lord frightened the giants and they abandon their mountain in abject terror. We need the faith of Caleb for the days we are now facing.

Strengthened by the Word of God, our little band of fighters faced this massive horde of gigantic warriors. As they moved forward for battle, the heavens opened and the light of God poured out like fire on the entire army of the enemy. When the light hit the darkness, every one of them shattered into millions of little pieces and became like dust which was quickly blown away by the four winds of God. The "Light of God" shed a great warmth over and through all the believers who had stood against the coldness of the enemy attack. The warmth of God's light came over us like a blanket which healed and restored every wounded soldier of God. Once again, we saw that all we have to do is "suit up" and "show up," and watch God defeat the enemy. Darkness cannot stand against the Light. The destruction of darkness is immediate and complete.

I pray that the light and life of God will cover you like a blanket in the cold air of the enemy's futile war against God and His saints. I pray that you will feel the warmth, receive the restoration, and be equipped to keep on standing in your faith. I pray that you will always remember that the battle has already been won. Yeshua ha Messiah has valiantly faced all the forces of darkness and death. He has emerged totally victorious. He is now in possession of the keys of death, hell, and the grave. His victory is our victory. We have already won! Amen!

Remember the words of Paul in Ephesians 6:10-13, *"Finally, my brethren, be strong in the Lord and in the power of His might. Put on the whole armor of God, that you may be able to stand against the wiles of the devil. For we do not wrestle against flesh and blood, but against principalities, against powers, against the rulers of the darkness of this age, against spiritual hosts of wickedness in the heavenly places. Therefore take up the whole armor of God, that you may be able to withstand in the evil day, and having done all, to stand."*

———————————

DAY 92

GIVE THE FATHER PRAISE

It is a beautiful morning in Heaven. The air is filled with expectancy and joy. Today, Father God will be praised around the world and the angels of heaven are ready to participate and add to the glory rising from earth. Can you feel that expectancy and joy? Are you ready to give Him praise?

This morning, I saw "Baruch ha Shem" (Bless the Lord! Or Praise the Lord!) written in the sky in Heaven. As I prayed and asked Father God to send word through the Holy Spirit about what would please Him and bless Yeshua ha Messiah today, I heard the Lord say, "Give praise to the Father!" Psalm 103:1-2, *"Bless the Name, O my soul; and all that is within me, bless His holy name! Bless the Lord, O my soul, and forget not all His benefits:"*

That seemed like an everyday thought. This is something we should be doing all day every day. But, somehow it meant more. Then the Holy Spirit revealed to me that this command should become more meaningful, more exciting, and more fulfilling every day. It never becomes routine or mundane. Every day it is more exciting to give Him praise! Every day it becomes more exciting to give him wholehearted worship and praise! Hallelujah!

Then I heard the Holy Spirit saying, "Give praise to the Lord! Not because He needs it! He likes it, but He doesn't need it. Praise Him because you need it. As you praise Him for who He is, you build up your love, appreciation, and faith in Him. As you praise Him for what He has done, you build up you belief system that He is a God who acts on the part of His people. He has answered your prayers in the past. He has been with you in the past. He has blessed you with favor and every spiritual blessing in the past, and you know that know that He will do that for you today and forever. Praise is your faith builder. Praise more and raise you faith, expectancy, and assurance!"

> *"My mouth shall tell of Your righteousness and Your salvation all the day, for I do not know their limits. I will go in the strength of the Lord GOD; I will make mention of Your righteousness, of Yours only. O God, You have taught me from my youth; and to this day I declare Your wondrous works. Now also when I am old and gray headed, O God, do not forsake me, until I declare Your strength to this generation, Your power to everyone who is to come. Also Your righteousness, O God, is very high, You who have done great things; O God, who is like You?"* (Psalm 71:15-19)

May you give Him wholehearted praise today! May it build you up in His Holy faith! May the praise you offer Him today give you encouragement and strength to face every challenge the day may bring! May your praise please Father God, bless Yeshua, and honor the Holy Spirit today! Amen!

DAY 93

TIME FOR A BREAKOUT

This morning I visited a room in Heaven filled with snow-globes of various sizes, shapes, and designs. The Lord was looking at the globes with sadness in His eyes. Then, He said, "It is in your nature to attempt to build little protective bubbles for yourself where you can feel safe and live in the illusion that you have control over your environment. Unfortunately, people actually lock all their troubles inside with themselves and lock out my power and gifts. You need to break out of your little protective spheres and walk in the destiny I have established for you. In your little spheres you lock out your ability to influence others for me and you lock out all that I have provided for you."

I have always been fascinated with snow globes and love to look at all the creative ways artists have made these unique works. I had never thought of them as somehow representing the way we attempt to establish little protective bubbles for ourselves. But, now it was very clear, and I began to think of the ways we do that. I remembered some of the globes with little homes in the woods where snow falls harmlessly and beautifully over the scene. There it was! The house was totally isolated from everyone on the outside. It might be a restful little vacation spot, but it was a very lonely permanent residence.

I remembered the globes with Christmas scenes. They are beautiful, but they limit life to one season with its special meaning, but everything else is shut out, and the richness of the entire cycle of life is lost. I remembered the globes with nativity scenes. Surely these are good globes because they focus on the gift of God in Jesus Christ. But, then I saw it. Jesus is never allowed to grow up and become the savior of the world in these little globes. In these bubbles, we many never have to face the blood and sacrifice, but we never get to the gift of eternal life.

In John 10:10 (NIV), we read how Jesus said, *"The thief comes only to steal and kill and destroy; I have come that they may have life, and have it to the full."* Our little protective bubbles attempt to lock out the enemy, but we also miss life in abundance, to the full, until it overflows. What we actually do is lock the enemy in where he can steal our life, our abundance, and our overflow. It is time to break out of our self-imposed prisons and live the abundant life God sent Jesus to give us. It is dangerous out here, but we have a promise: *"You are of God, little children, and have overcome them, because He who is in you is greater than he who is in the world."* (1 John 4:4)

May God bless you with an open heaven instead of a protective bubble! May the Lord draw you out of your safety zone and into the battle for the kingdom of God! May God open your eyes to see the awesome work He has planned, and your part in it! May God bless you with the indwelling Holy Spirit who is greater than all that the enemy can muster against you! May you receive a breakthrough which moves you to a higher level and a greater anointing for the fulfillment of God's purpose in your life! Amen!

DAY 94

LIVING WATER IS FLOWING

This morning, I waited a long time to receive a message from Heaven. I was in a vision, but could not see clearly. There were dark clouds in front of me, and I was only occasionally seeing glimpses of the things of Heaven. I continued to pray for the Lord to open my spiritual eyes and bind the enemy's attempts to block my view of Heaven. I asked the Holy Spirit to unstop my spiritual ears and open them wide so that I could clearly hear what the Lord is saying today.

After a lengthy time of praying in the spirit, my spiritual eyes were suddenly opened and I was standing near a raging river flowing over a vast waterfall much larger than Niagara Falls. The water was pounding the rocks below and great billows of white mist arose making the scene in front of the falls appear to be great clouds in the sky. In the distance I could see the Temple in heaven and understood that the water was flowing from the Temple. It was amazing because it was getting deeper and swifter the further it flowed from the temple. I stood in amazement and awe at the power and provision from God. I remembered John's words in Revelation 22:1, "*And he showed me a pure river of water of life, clear as crystal, proceeding from the throne of God and of the Lamb.*"

As I stood watching, I heard the Lord say, "Cleansing, refreshing, healing, and renewing power are flowing forth from the throne." I had asked in my prayers to come boldly before the throne of grace. I had been expecting something a little closer than this. However, I was standing in the power flow from the throne of grace (at a distance) and it was awesome. I stood receiving a misty covering over me and embraced the

260

cleansing, refreshing, healing, and renewing flow from my Father God! It was so wonderful, and I wanted you to experience it too.

Then the Holy Spirit directed my view a little further down below where I was standing, and I saw a huge portal in Heaven opened over the earth. This amazing flow was pouring down through an open heaven and flowing in great power and abundance on all those on earth who were open to receive it. In that moment, I knew that you were also receiving this flow in abundance and I prayed for you to receive the "cleansing, refreshing, healing, and renewing power flowing forth from the throne."

As I looked at the earth, it was covered with darkness, deception, and wickedness. But, now it was being washed, cleansed, refreshed, healed and renewed. As I watched I noticed that the flow was not spilling directly on the earth. It was flowing through us. The rivers of living water were flowing into us and through us – and then into the world. John 7:37-38, *"On the last day, that great day of the feast, Jesus stood and cried out, saying, "If anyone thirsts, let him come to Me and drink. He who believes in Me, as the Scripture has said, out of his heart will flow rivers of living water."*

As I watched, the world was changing. The darkness and filth were being washed away in a great flood. It was then that I remembered many of the messages from heaven this month about the destiny God was planning for us – the provision He had prepared for us – and the great opportunities for this coming season. Then I understood that the dark clouds and difficulty I had seen in Heaven this morning were images speaking to me of the troublesome time we have gone through, but now we are at the dawn of the "new thing" God is releasing to the world.

Are you ready to receive the flow from Heaven? Then reach out and receive the awesome cleansing, the fresh baptism, the new anointing for healing and restoration! Let it flow into you, do its work in you, and then flow forth to do its work in the world. God is blessing you so that you can be a blessing (Genesis 12). May you receive all that the Lord has for you today and forever! Amen!

DAY 95

YOUR LIGHT HAS COME

T his morning as I was crying out to the Lord face down in my worship room, I asked that He would tell us what we could do today to honor, bless, and please the Father, the Son, and the Holy Spirit. As I prayed, I was carried in the Spirit to heaven and stood at the edge of a very large portal looking down on the earth. The earth seemed to be wrapped in darkness. I remembered the words of Isaiah 60:1-3, *"Arise, shine; for your light has come! And the glory of the Lord is risen upon you. For behold, the darkness shall cover the earth, and deep darkness the people; but the LORD will arise over you, and His glory will be seen upon you. The Gentiles shall come to your light, and kings to the brightness of your rising."*

As I looked at the darkness of the earth, a huge light appeared in the sky over the earth. It was of a powder blue color and was in the shape of a cross which was at least twice the diameter of the earth. A great light was shining over the deep darkness of the earth. Then I heard the Lord saying, "Don't get caught up in the tinsel! Don't get caught up in the images of wrapping paper, decorations, and lights! I created you to learn and receive through images. That's why I commanded you *"You shall not make for yourself a carved image—any likeness of anything that is in heaven above, or that is in the earth beneath, or that is in the water under the earth;"* (Exodus 20:4) Images will distract your mind and lead you away from me! So, keep your eyes fixed on Jesus and the cross He endured for you." My mind quickly went to Hebrews 12:2-3, *"looking unto Jesus, the author and finisher of our faith, who for the joy that was set before Him endured the cross, despising the shame, and has sat*

263

down at the right hand of the throne of God. For consider Him who endured such hostility from sinners against Himself, lest you become weary and discouraged in your souls."

The Lord was not telling us to quit celebrating Christmas or to quit putting up decorations and wrapping gifts. He was making it clear that we need to focus most on the main message of the season. It is all about Jesus and what He did for us on the cross. He didn't ask us to remember His birth (although that is a good thing). He asked us to remember that His body was broken and His blood was shed for the redemption of our sin and the establishment of the kingdom of God on earth. Go ahead with your celebrations, and at the same time remember the gospel of the kingdom this Christmas. Remember why He came. 1 John 3:8b, *"For this purpose the Son of God was manifested, that He might destroy the works of the devil."* One of the main works of the devil is to distract us from focusing on Father God and what He has done for us through His Son, Jesus the Anointed One.

May we cast off every veil of the enemy this season and keep our eyes focused on Jesus! May the primary symbol of the season remain the cross! May the light of Jesus shine into every area of darkness we encounter in our world! May you remember the words of John 8:12, *"Then Jesus spoke to them again, saying, "I am the light of the world. He who follows Me shall not walk in darkness, but have the light of life."* Indeed, "your light has come" and the "glory of the Lord is risen upon you." And, this light has done something remarkable in us. It has changed us into carriers of the Light. Jesus also said, *"You are the light of the world. A city that is set on a hill cannot be hidden. Nor do they light a lamp and put it under a basket, but on a lampstand, and it gives light to all who are in the house. Let your light so shine before men, that they may see your good works and glorify your Father in heaven."* (Matthew 5:14-16)

May you carry the light in a way that will honor the Father, bless the Son, and please the Holy Spirit! May you be a bright light in a world filled with deep darkness as you represent the "father of lights" this season and every season! Amen! Reflect again on the deep meaning of Isaiah 60:1, *"Arise, shine; for your light has come! And the glory of the Lord is risen upon you."* Hallelujah! Baruch ha Shem!

MORE SEED FOR SOWERS

This morning, I looked up in the spirit and saw an open heaven. I always appreciate seeing an open heaven. As I looked at it, I wondered what the Lord was about to do. Then, I saw the Lord tearing it open wider and wider. I remembered Mark 1:10 (NIV), "*As Jesus was coming up out of the water, he saw heaven being torn open and the Spirit descending on him like a dove.*" The Lord didn't just make a little hole in heaven or open a door or a window. He literally tore it open, and nowhere in scripture do we read about him closing or sewing up the opening. The heavens are still open over those who are in Christ! And, that was what I was seeing this morning.

As I watched the Lord tearing it open wider, I heard Him say, "I want to pour out more from my storehouse on those who are faithful to receive it, and use it for the kingdom. My storehouse has not diminished. It is not dependent on the earth's economy. Remember how Isaac sowed in a time of famine and reaped a hundred fold. That is what I want to do for my people now. But, who is ready to receive it?"

Many people have never learned to operate under an open heaven. They have never learned to just reach up and take what God has for them. Many people have embraced poverty as some sort of virtue, but according to the Word of God, poverty is a result of the curse. In Christ, we are not under the curse. We are under the blessing of Abraham whom God made very rich. Can we receive this word from the Lord? Can we embrace the concept of an open heaven? Can we go further and open up to receive all that God has for us today and every day?

As I reflected on these ideas, I heard the Lord asking, "Did you catch that part about Isaac sowing?" So many people miss that part. They expect to receive without taking any steps on their own. This is not a biblical thought. Sowing always precedes reaping. Malachi 3:10, "'*Bring all the tithes into the storehouse, that there may be food in My house, and try Me now in this,*' *says the Lord of hosts,* '*If I will not open for you the windows of heaven and pour out for you such blessing that there will not be room enough to receive it.*'" Bringing in the tithe and sowing our offerings provides the material from which God multiplies our seed and returns a great harvest to us. Isaac sowed first and then reaped a hundred fold.

Isaiah received this promise; "*For as the rain comes down, and the snow from heaven, and do not return there, but water the earth, and make it bring forth and bud, that it may give seed to the sower and bread to the eater, so shall My word be that goes forth from My mouth; It shall not return to Me void, but it shall accomplish what I please, and it shall prosper in the thing for which I sent it.*" (Isaiah 55:10-11)

I believe that Paul had received this same revelation when he wrote 2 Corinthians 9:10-15, "*Now may He who supplies seed to the sower, and bread for food, supply and multiply the seed you have sown and increase the fruits of your righteousness, while you are enriched in everything for all liberality, which causes thanksgiving through us to God. For the administration of this service not only supplies the needs of the saints, but also is abounding through many thanksgivings to God, while, through the proof of this ministry, they glorify God for the obedience of your confession to the gospel of Christ, and for your liberal sharing with them and all men, and by their prayer for you, who long for you because of the exceeding grace of God in you. Thanks be to God for His indescribable gift!*"

We have all these testimonies, and yet many people find this difficult to understand and apply. What is often missed is the Lord's desire to bless us, multiply our seed, give us a great harvest, provide help for others through us, and produce a harvest of thanksgiving for Himself. Great poverty does not lead to great thanksgiving. Great prosperity results in great thanksgiving to the Lord. My prayer for you today as you stand under an open heaven is the prayer of John in 3 John 1:2, *"Beloved, I pray that you may prosper in all things and be in health, just as your soul prospers."* God's prosperity is for spirit, soul, and body, and I pray that you will receive it in abundance and be filled to overflowing with thanksgiving unto the Lord! Amen!

DAY 97

HUBBLE HUMBLED ME

This morning standing before the Throne of Grace, I asked the Lord what we could do to please Him, bless Jesus, and honor the Holy Spirit. I waited to hear something new and exciting, but I simply heard, "There is too much 'me focus' (meaning that we are focusing on ourselves more than Him) in this holiday." It seemed cliché to go over this ground which is being covered in thousands of sermons in churches around the world. But, somehow this is very important in Heaven today. Every year we go through these thoughts of keeping Christ in Christmas, and we pay lip service to the idea. We put up a few more nativity scenes and think we are doing well. But, have we really changed in the core of our being? So, what are you giving to Jesus this year for His birthday?

After Christmas the typical question is, "What did you get for Christmas?" That is usually followed quickly by, "Did you get what you really wanted?" How did it all become about us? When did that begin, and how did we get it so far away from what the Father did for us through Yeshua? We have become so accustomed to asking these questions that I don't know if they mean very much to us?

As I thought about this, I was suddenly looking into the vastness of the universe. It was as if I had a built-in Hubble Telescope giving me views of galaxies millions of light years away. I love to go to the NASA website and look at the pictures from Hubble, and this was an awesome time in the Lord. I saw again the Whirlpool Galaxy which is as far out as we have been able to see so far. In the center of this galaxy is a black hole which appears through the Hubble Telescope to be a blue circle with a cross in the center. As far out as we can see, God has given us the sign of the cross. As I was taken in by the massiveness of the universe, I realized once again that our God is bigger than we have ever imagined. The universe is massive and earth is so tiny by comparison. The Holy Spirit led me to Psalm 8:3-4, *"When I consider Your heavens, the work of Your fingers, the moon and the stars, which You have ordained, What is man that You are mindful of him, and the son of man that You visit him?"* These words took on new meaning this morning. We are so small and He is huge beyond our ability to understand.

Looking at the Universe and considering our tiny little planet and thinking of how small we are on this blue planet, what are we that the Creator God of the Universe would consider us? Psalm 33:6 says, *"By the word of the* Lord *the heavens were made, and all the host of them by the breath of His mouth."* How does the Lord who speaks the Universe into being – the God who breathes out stars, planets, and moons – consider such insignificant beings worthy of His time and attention? Yet, according to Psalm 8:5-9, *"For You have made him a little lower than the angels (Elohim), and You have crowned him with glory and honor. You have made him to have dominion over the works of Your hands; You have put all things under his feet, all sheep and oxen—even the beasts of the field, the birds of the air, and the fish of the sea that pass through the paths of the seas. O Lord, our Lord, how excellent is Your name in all the earth!"*

I was once again reminded of who He is and who I am in Christ Jesus. I went back to the Hubble website, and found this headline of the day, "Hubble Supernova Bubble Resembles Holiday Ornament." Check it out! I did. Is that awesome? God has decorated the Universe with a gigantic Christmas ornament to honor His Son. It is all about Him! That ornament in the heavens makes all of my decorations seem tiny and trivial. Yet, God wants to bring us into this celebration. After all, He did it all for us. My heart is alive with joy and expectancy this morning. What will our star breathing God do next?

How can we give someone like this the honor He is due? How will we honor Him today, throughout the season, and forever? He is due so much praise, adoration, loyalty, honor, and majesty! Hallelujah! Let's focus on Him forever! So, what are you giving to Yeshua for Christmas this year?

DAY 98

KNOW YOUR AUTHORITY

This morning as I prayed to hear from heaven, I was especially focused on a desire to avoid grieving the Holy Spirit. The Holy Spirit is very sensitive to hurt and often grieves over those who are not walking closely with God. I have a great desire to never grieve the Holy Spirit again. So, I actively seek correction, discipline, and admonishment. I was concerned this morning that others are close to grieving the Holy Spirit in this season. So, I cried out to know what we must do to please, bless, and honor the Father, the Son and the Holy Spirit.

As I prayed, I was lifted up into the second heaven where I saw a very large black bird holding a pearl in his left set of talons. The pearl was glowing and very bright. The bird (the devil) snarled a dare at me. He said, "Take it if you think you can." I was tempted to reach out and take it, but I realized that I would be doing that without the authority of the Lord. So, I held back my hand and prayed for the seven spirits of God to be released to deal with the bird and take back the pearl. I was immediately carried up to the third heaven.

The Lord spoke to me and said that I had done well to discern the absence of authority and refrain from trying to take something out of the devil's hand in his territory. I looked and saw the Lord Jesus with the seven Spirits of God, and I prayed that He would release the seven Spirits to deal with the enemy. The seven Spirits immediately went out to do the work of the Lord. The Lord then guided me through a teaching which I had received before in a different context. He said, "Many people are warring in the second heaven without authority. They are being hurt and experiencing great loss. Some have even lost their lives." The Lord reminded me of Jude 1:9, "*Yet Michael the archangel, in contending with the devil, when he disputed about the body of Moses, dared not bring against him a reviling accusation, but said, "The Lord rebuke you!"*" When we are dealing with principalities, we need to learn to let the Holy Spirit do His work and only do what we are commissioned and commanded to do.

The Lord has given us awesome power and protection and we must learn to use it wisely. I was reminded again of Paul's words in Ephesians 6:10-13, "*Finally, my brethren, be strong in the Lord and in the power of His might. Put on the whole armor of God, that you may be able to stand against the wiles of the devil. For we do not wrestle against flesh and blood, but against principalities, against powers, against the rulers of the darkness of this age, against spiritual hosts of wickedness in the heavenly places. Therefore take up the whole armor of God, that you may be able to withstand in the evil day, and having done all, to stand.*" We must always remember who we are fighting against and the rules of engagement. Let the Holy Spirit do your fighting against the "spiritual hosts of wickedness in the heavenly places."

God has provided awesome protection. So, put on your armor daily and take your stand against the enemy. Notice that the armor Paul talks about is defensive in nature. We have all we need to stand our ground for the Lord. Ephesians 6:14-18, "*Stand therefore, having girded your waist with truth, having put on the breastplate of righteousness, and having shod your feet with the preparation of the gospel of peace; above all, taking the shield of faith with which you will be able to quench all the fiery darts of the wicked one. And take the helmet of salvation, and the sword of the Spirit, which is the word of God; praying always with all prayer and supplication in the Spirit, being watchful to this end with all perseverance and supplication for all the saints*" We also have great power through praying in the Spirit in accordance with the Word of God.

Isaiah gave us a great advent message in chapter eleven verses 1-4, *"There shall come forth a Rod from the stem of Jesse, and a Branch shall grow out of his roots. The Spirit of the Lord shall rest upon Him, the Spirit of wisdom and understanding, the Spirit of counsel and might, the Spirit of knowledge and of the fear of the Lord. His delight is in the fear of the Lord, and He shall not judge by the sight of His eyes, nor decide by the hearing of His ears; But with righteousness He shall judge the poor, and decide with equity for the meek of the earth; He shall strike the earth with the rod of His mouth, and with the breath of His lips He shall slay the wicked."* The Lord will use the sword in His mouth to strike the earth and destroy the wicked. Revelation 19:15, *"Now out of His mouth goes a sharp sword, that with it He should strike the nations. And He Himself will rule them with a rod of iron. He Himself treads the winepress of the fierceness and wrath of Almighty God."* May the Lord give you wisdom and revelation, counsel and might, and knowledge of the fear of the Lord! I thank Father God for sending Yeshua to win the victory for us! Amen!

DAY 99

WORSHIP OPENS THE FLOW

Worship in heaven is awesome today with millions of angels joining our worship to give praise, glory, honor, and majesty to our Father God! As I worshipped in awe this morning I asked what would please the Father, bless the Son, and honor the Holy Spirit today. The Lord answered, "Give the praise and worship due His name!" In my spirit, I heard the words of 1 Chronicles 16:29, *"Give to the LORD the glory due His name; bring an offering, and come before Him. Oh, worship the LORD in the beauty of holiness!"* As amazing as it sounds, our praise and worship blesses the Father, the Son and the Holy Spirit. It is a gift of God that we are given an ability to bless His name. Then I heard the Lord say, "Whether in a large group, a small group, or alone, your praise and worship blesses Him!"

My focus was totally on the worship and praise, and I felt like I was in touch with all the praise coming up from earth today as well as the praise in Heaven. It was such an amazing feeling. Then I saw the glory of God (like a whirlwind of fire rotating counter-clockwise) dancing in response to the worship. It was so wonderful to see the Father responding to our feeble attempts to give Him the worship He is due. Then He began to release a flow of impartation in waves. Each wave seemed to permeate my entire being. It was an impartation of power, life, provision, and everything my heart could desire. The feeling I experienced while receiving this impartation was wonderful beyond description. Then I heard the Lord say, "Worship is the key to unlock the flow of impartation from heaven! Whatever your situation may be, worship will open the heavens to respond to your need. Worship is more powerful than begging or pleading. Worship and let the flow of God's provision be released into your spirit, soul, and body!"

The writer of Hebrews reminds us that the gift of discernment is built up through use. *"But solid food belongs to those who are of full age, that is, those who by reason of use have their senses exercised to discern both good and evil."* (Hebrews 5:14). Worship, like all the Spiritual Gifts is strengthened through use. So, I worshipped more intensely. As I worshipped the Lord, I experienced such joy, strength, comfort, and assurance. I want to worship more and stay connected to the flow of God's Spirit at all times. I think this is what Paul was referring to in Ephesians 5:18-20, *"And do not be drunk with wine, in which is dissipation; but be filled with the Spirit, speaking to one another in psalms and hymns and spiritual songs, singing and making melody in your heart to the Lord, giving thanks always for all things to God the Father in the name of our Lord Jesus Christ,"*

Again in Colossians 3:15-17 (NIV), Paul said, *"Let the peace of Christ rule in your hearts, since as members of one body you were called to peace. And be thankful. Let the word of Christ dwell in you richly as you teach and admonish one another with all wisdom, and as you sing psalms, hymns and spiritual songs with gratitude in your hearts to God. And whatever you do, whether in word or deed, do it all in the name of the Lord Jesus, giving thanks to God the Father through him."*

May your heart be filled with thanksgiving, praise, and worship today! May your worship open the flow of impartation from heaven! May your continuous worship, praise, and thanksgiving keep the flow of God's provision in your life and ministry! May the Lord release His power over you now as you read this and meditate on what He has in store for you! Amen!

DAY 100

MONDAY MERCIES

This morning, something unusual happened as I lay face down in worship. I was playing worship music on a wide-screen TV through my computer. As I was praying, the sound stopped. A program downloaded an update and rebooted my computer. When this happens, the program usually stops at the log in screen waiting for me to enter a password. Then I have to restart the worship program and manually select widescreen projection. So, I just continued to pray in the atmosphere of silence. I asked the Lord to tell me what heaven is saying today, and I clearly heard the Lord saying, "Monday Mercies! Many people dread Monday and speak curses into the day. But I am filling this day with mercies!"

At this point in my prayer, the computer finished rebooting and started the worship music in widescreen mode just as the worship song proclaimed that we should lift our voices in praise! The sound was so loud and startling that I jumped in surprise. Then I asked the Lord if this was from Him and He said, "Yes!" I knew that the answer to my prayer about what would please the Father, bless the Son, and honor the Holy Spirit was for us to raise our voices and proclaim "out of Zion's hill Salvation comes!" If you want to open the portals in Heaven to receive the mercies God has in store for you, raise your voice and proclaim that Jesus brought salvation to Zion's hill! Amen?

As the worship music continued, the words of the praise music resonated in my soul more than ever. It reminded me that we are not looking for another baby in a manger. We are waiting expectantly for the arrival of the King of kings in all

His power and glory! We are waiting for a conquering savior king to arrive on a white horse and destroy all His enemies with the sword in His mouth (the Word of God). Hallelujah! He is coming! As the old spiritual proclaims, "Soon and very Soon we're going to see the King!" Hallelujah!

We are in a season of joy and expectancy. What are we expecting? On our visit to Israel, we had the opportunity to pray at the Western Wall. It was a very meaningful experience for me, but I realized that I had missed something when Kevin Basconi announced that he had an angelic encounter at the wall. I know that he lives with this expectation and it is so often fulfilled for him. I came under conviction. I had not expected anything supernatural. I had only expected to pray in a special place. I received what I expected and Kevin received what he expected. So, I went back to pray with expectancy to receive a supernatural encounter and all I can say is "Wow!" God did not disappoint me. Jesus said to the centurion, "*Go your way; and as you have believed, so let it be done for you.' And his servant was healed that same hour.*" (Matthew 8:13) If you receive what you believe today, what will it be?

We must increase our level of expectancy! We serve an awesome God who promises to send out new mercies every day. Lamentations 3:22-23, "*Through the Lord's mercies we are not consumed, because His compassions fail not. They are new every morning; great is Your faithfulness.*" Don't miss out on His Monday Mercies! Raise your level of expectation, today and every day. Believe that today God's favor will be with you and bless everything your hand touches! Believe that you are extremely blessed and highly favored! Expect it! Confess it! And, receive it in the name of Jesus! Amen!

SUMMARY

This morning in worship, I saw a huge portal into heaven and I pressed in — to move through it. I was immediately lifted by the Spirit into heaven where I suddenly went into a vision. In the vision, I saw a predawn scene over the people of earth. The clouds in the sky were dark and the mountains in the distance blocked the earliest rays of light. The words of Isaiah 60:1-4b came into my mind, *"Arise, shine; for your light has come! And the glory of the Lord is risen upon you. For behold, the darkness shall cover the earth, and deep darkness the people; But the Lord will arise over you, and His glory will be seen upon you. The Gentiles shall come to your light, and kings to the brightness of your rising. "Lift up your eyes all around, and see:"*

As I watched, the light continued to rise over the earth, but to my surprise many people avoided seeing it. They hid their faces from the light. They focused on the darkness and refused to see the light. I wanted to shout out to all of them, "Can't you see! The light of God has risen! Look up and see!" I was pleased to see that many people longed for the light to penetrate their darkness, and they were straining to receive the light. I joined in with this group. As we watched, the scene changed as a powerful beam of light came from above. This light overwhelmed the light of the sun rising over the horizon. It was a powerful light from heaven that was shattering the darkness, and in the center of the light was Jesus. He was poised to return again as the light of the world. I remembered again the words of John in Revelation 22:20, *"He who testifies to these things says, 'Surely I am coming quickly.' Amen. Even so, come, Lord Jesus!"* Then I cried out, "Even so, come quickly, Lord Jesus!"

This vision suddenly ended and I was in the midst of a second vision. I saw a great city with many lights shining in the last moments of a pre-dawn morning. The city was located below mountains which surrounded it on all sides. I was on a mountain west of the city as I watched the sun rise over the peaks on the east side. Because of the mountain peaks, there was a mixture of light and darkness over the city. When the people saw the light rising, some went out into the streets to welcome the light and warmth of this new morning, but others hurried into their houses and turned off their lights. They wanted to hide from the light instead of welcoming this gift from heaven.

Then I realized that the two visions were the same. As this realization settled into my mind, the Holy Spirit reminded me of John 1:5, *"And the light shines in the darkness, and the darkness did not comprehend it."* Jesus shed even more light on this when He said, *"And this is the condemnation, that the light has come into the world, and men loved darkness rather than light, because their deeds were evil. For everyone practicing evil hates the light and does not come to the light, lest his deeds should be exposed. But he who does the truth comes to the light, that his deeds may be clearly seen, that they have been done in God."* (John 3:19-21) The irony is that the people who need the light the most are the ones who are hiding from it.

I don't know about you, but I am praying for more light to shine into the darkness of this world and into my own spirit. I want to see Jesus and experience all that God has for us through Him. I want the Holy Spirit to reveal the light more and more. I want to embrace the Light of the World! I want to be obedient to the Lord Jesus so that He can come to me and abide in me! How about you? Will you run toward the light or hide from it? Look once more at what Jesus said in John 8:12, *"Then Jesus spoke to them again, saying, "I am the light of the world. He who follows Me shall not walk in darkness, but have the light of life."*

John summed the situation up very well in John 1:10-13, *"He was in the world, and the world was made through Him, and the world did not know Him. He came to His own, and His own did not receive Him. But as many as received Him, to them He gave the right to become children of God, to those who believe in His name: who were born, not of blood, nor of the will of the flesh, nor of the will of man, but of God."* May we all walk in the light so that we can receive this promise and become the "children of God!" Embrace the Light of God! He came to shatter the darkness around you and escort you into the kingdom of light, love, blessing, and favor! Now is your time to receive it. Amen!

PRAYER TO ACCEPT JESUS

Jesus, I am so tired of living in deep darkness and in the deception of the world. I believe that you died for my sin and that Father God raised you from the dead. I want to walk in your light and be part of your Kingdom of Light! I am confessing with my mouth that you are Lord in my life. Please forgive me for living apart from you and for not welcoming you in the past! Forgive all my sin and live in me as you promised! Help me to live in obedience so that Father God can also live in me! Fill my heart with your love and teach me to love others as you have loved me! Amen and Amen!

BONUS MESSAGES

CHRISTMAS EVE IN HEAVEN

L ast night we were in worship until after 11:15 p.m. I experienced an angelic visitation followed by a visit from Yeshua
who released a great blessing and an impartation of His Spirit.
Everyone present received an anointing for the opening of their
spiritual eyes and ears in order to see and hear from the Lord. The
Lord came bearing gifts for us! Wow! It was an awesome time.

This morning, as I was face down in our worship room, I was
immediately caught up in a vision of the Lord. In front of me was
a wall covered in a mosaic of clipped out advertisements showing
all the things people ask for as gifts at Christmas. In addition,
there were pictures (as from the society page of a newspaper)
of people standing together; dressed in expensive clothing; and
gathered around their new luxury cars. Crowds of people had
gathered around this wall and were gazing at the pictures; trying
to see all the things that earthly pleasures could provide.

The Spirit of God pulled me further back from the wall so
that I could see that it (this wall) was merely one of the props
on a stage which had been prepared for some great production.
People had gotten so focused on the props that they were no
longer aware that the actors were ready to come out and begin
the play. The play was being delayed because people had
crowded onto the stage to gaze at the pictures on the props. I
heard the Lord say, "Don't get caught up in the trappings which
are merely props on the stage! Keep your eyes focused on what
is about to happen. Don't miss out on what I am about to do!"

Suddenly stage hands (angels) brought out a magnificent throne which appeared to be constructed of living stones radiating with God's glory. Powerful angels gathered around the throne awaiting the arrival of the one with the leading role. Then He appeared. It was Yeshua in magnificent robes with an awesome crown on His head. He took His place on the throne, and prepared to rule and reign over the earth. I was appalled to see crowds still on the stage; gathered around the props; and staring at the pictures as if they were going to suddenly jump out as their personal gifts. I wanted to cry out, "Don't you see what is happening? Can't you see that King Jesus is here in our midst?" Jesus continued on as if the people were not there. Their failure to see did not stop what He planned to do. He raised His hand in blessing to those who had bowed before Him.

Suddenly, I was aware that I had a gift in my hand. It was a small, thin gift wrapped package. As I opened it, I found a small sized zip-locked plastic bag containing some sort of cloth. As I opened it, reached inside, and pulled the cloth out, I saw that it was crimson red and very moist. It was filled with the shed blood of Jesus. It was the gift of redemption which many were seeing as small compared to the luxury cars, expensive furs, and electronic gadgets in the pictures on the props. It was small in size but great beyond description for those who received it. I took the cloth out and anointed my head with the blood of Jesus. I held it to my heart and embraced the greatest of all gifts. I was filled with joy, contentment, and gratitude.

My focus shifted and I saw you there holding the same small gift wrapped package. I watched as you opened it, and in amazement embraced this best of all possible gifts. Then I heard the Lord say again, "Keep your eyes on what is truly valuable! Keep your eyes on Jesus! Keep your eyes on what He has done for you! And, share this gift with others to honor Him and glorify me!" This is the greatest gift you can receive and give in this season! Amen?

May you receive what the Lord has paid such a great price to give! May you pass it on to as many others as possible! May you help those focused on the props to see what the real event is all about! May we give the Lord what He so richly deserves our loyalty, gratitude, and willing service in His kingdom! May we give the nations as disciples back to Him! Amen!!!

LOOKING TOWARD A NEW YEAR

This morning, I asked the Lord, "Is there a Word from Heaven about the coming year? I want to hear what to expect in this new season! Jesus promised that the Holy Spirit would guide us into all truth, and I am placing a claim on that promise. So, Father God, please give us a Word from heaven today!" I was reminded by the Holy Spirit of a previous message to meditate on the character of God. I quickly reflected on the Psalms I read this morning and what they said about Father God's character. After doing this, I became certain that His character was to disclose His plans to His prophets. At this point, I was carried in the Spirit to an open heaven. At first, I could not tell if I was above it looking down or below it looking up. Then it became clear. My view of the open heaven was alternating between below and above. Then I heard the Lord saying, "The new year will be a season of breakthrough! Things prophesied and hindered will be released and made manifest!"

I meditated on that promise and then by faith made it mine. Then the Lord spoke again saying, "This will be a year of breakthrough! Increase your level of expectation!" I have received this teaching over and over this year, and believe that it is critical to our walk in the new season. Remember the words of Jesus to the centurion, *"Then Jesus said to the centurion, 'Go your way; and as you have believed, so let it be done for you.' And his servant was healed that same hour."* (Matthew 8:13) I have learned this lesson and I am still learning it.

What is your expectation for the coming season of the Lord? If you know that you will receive what you believe then ask yourself, "Am I believing for enough?" I don't think we have faith for as much as He is willing to give. I am hearing many who are expecting to see great trouble, persecution, and lack in the coming year. They are making statements of faith and decrees for this outcome. However, I am believing in break-through. I am believing that God is going to make manifest those things He has prophesied. I am believing that the one who has hindered the fulfillment is being moved out of the way. I am expecting something great to happen very soon. In fact, I am believing that many great and wonderful things are going to happen in the next season. I am also standing on another promise: "But as it is written: *"Eye has not seen, nor ear heard, nor have entered into the heart of man the things which God has prepared for those who love Him."* (1 Corinthians 2:9)

God has prepared more for you than you have ever thought or imagined! Are you ready to receive it? Listen again to what the Lord said, "This season will be a year of breakthrough! Increase your level of expectation!" May you ask and imagine far beyond your normal level! May you then receive even more than that! May you continue to raise your level of expectation as your level of faith increases!

Then I looked again at the open heaven from beneath it. As I watched, the Lord released a firestorm of His glory. It was pouring out in great abundance for all those who believed. Then His Shekinah glory poured out from heaven to bless those who are expecting Him to dwell with them. As I continued to watch a green glory cloud of financial release flowed from the open heaven. This was followed by a greater anointing for gifts of healings. I saw body parts being released for creative miracles. Impartation came forth for signs and wonders to accompany the preaching of the gospel of the kingdom. How much of this are you expecting? Expect much more! God is releasing so much more than we have asked or imagined. Amen!

NEW YEAR'S EVE MESSAGE

This morning as I was praising Father God for who He is, my prayer was interrupted by a vision. I found myself standing in a video store looking at the rows and rows of DVDs and Videos. I began to ask if this was of the Lord. It seemed odd that it would come in the middle of my praise time. I wondered if my prayer was repetitive and perhaps I was boring the Lord. We listened to a great message last night on giving and receiving honor from sons to fathers and fathers to sons (mothers and daughters too). This had touched on issues that are sensitive and I did much processing during that time. These things were still on my mind and it was as if the Lord was saying: "I have chosen to forget the failures. So, don't remind me. Let it go and move on!" Hebrews 8:12, *"For I will be merciful to their unrighteousness, and their sins and their lawless deeds I will remember no more."* I stopped thinking of these things and looked at the videos as I waited for the Holy Spirit to guide me in understanding what I was seeing.

Very shortly the Holy Spirit directed my attention more closely to the titles on the videos. They were not from Hollywood or old TV shows. They were the stories of the lives of those who had followed the Lord and ministered in His name. The Lord said, "Nothing you have done for Me or the kingdom is ever forgotten. Nothing you have done for me has been wasted or lost." Even if you have not seen the fruit of your ministry, your words and works did not come back void. Everything is stored in the memory bank of the Father. Remember His words given in Isaiah 55:11, *"So shall My word be that goes forth from My mouth; It shall not return to Me void, But it shall accomplish what I please, And it shall prosper in the thing for which I sent it."*

Still processing last night's session, I wondered if all the failures to honor fathers, mothers, sons, and daughters were on the videos. I wondered if the failure to receive honor from fathers, mothers, sons, and daughters were recorded on the videos. Is

287

there a record here which the Lord holds on to and later uses to discipline or punish us? As I pondered this, the Lord reminded me again, "Those things you have given over to me, I have chosen to forget. These are the memories of your love, service, worship and praise." That was a relief! The Lord doesn't waste time as we do on negatives or things that can hinder or limit our creativity and service today. Amen! Thank you, Father!

As I looked at the videos, I thought there must be hundreds and hundreds of stories here. As this thought came into my mind, lights were turned on so that I could see more and more rows. I thought there must be thousands and thousands. Then more lights came on and I could see more of the vastness of this "memory bank" of the Lord. I thought there must be millions and millions of stories here. Then I saw more and the numbers went into billions. I began to feel really overwhelmed at the thought that the Father keeps all of this in His memory all the time. What an awesome Father God! Amen?

Then the Holy Spirit led me down an aisle. As we walked, I became aware that I was moving through paper thin layers of memories. When I stopped, the layer began to play out as if I was part of that memory. I stopped at a few places where the memories of people I knew or have studied were stored. As I stood in certain places of memory, I felt a desire to honor those individuals welling up in me. What an awesome thought! God is storing the memories that inspire honor.

Now, seeing what the Father is doing, I know what I must be doing. If I do what I see the Father doing, I will be giving more honor and respect to these father and mothers in ministry every day. Wow! Thank you Lord for adding a new layer of revelation and knowledge to the teaching I received last night. Most of all, I was inspired to give honor to Father God, Yeshua ha Messiah, and the Holy Spirit. My praise was no longer repetitive or routine. It was filled with honor for my Father God; my Lord Jesus; and my ever present friend, the Holy Spirit. Amen!

OTHER BOOKS BY THIS AUTHOR

"A Warrior's Guide to the Seven Spirits of God" - Part 1: Basic Training, by James A. Durham, Copyright © James A. Durham, printed by Xulon Press, August 2011.

"A Warrior's Guide to the Seven Spirits of God" - Part 2: Advanced Individual Training, by James A. Durham, Copyright © James A. Durham, printed by Xulon Press, August 2011.

"Beyond the Ancient Door" – Free to Move About the Heavens, by James A. Durham, Copyright © James A. Durham, printed by Xulon Press, April 2012.

"Restoring Foundations for Intercessor Warriors" by James A. Durham, Copyright © James A. Durham, printed by Xulon Press, May 2012.

"Gatekeepers Arise!" by James A. Durham, Copyright © James A. Durham, printed by Xulon Press, February 2013

"Seven Levels of Glory" by James A. Durham, Copyright © James A. Durham, printed by Xulon Press, June 2013